Live, Love, Lead

Ten Simple Skills to Transform Stress

CYNTHIA L. MOORE

The author thanks the following publishers and authors for permission to reprint material copyrighted or controlled by them.

Quote from the *Daily Word* for October 27, 2013, reprinted with permission of Unity, publisher of *Daily Word*.

Quote from *A Course in Miracles are from the second Edition*, 1985, © Foundation for Inner Peace, P.O. Box 598, Mill Valley, CA 94942-0598, www.acim.org and info@acim.org.

Quote from *The Yoga Sutras of Patanjali*, by Sri Swami Satchidananda, Integral Yoga Publications, 1990.

Quotes from *Toughness Training for Life*. New York: Plume, 1994. Permission granted by Sam Moore, Permissions Department, Penguin Group.

Illness-Wellness Continuum © 1981, 1988, 2004 by John W. Travis, MD. Reproduced with permission, from *Wellness Workbook: How to Achieve Enduring Health and Vitality*, 3rd ed., by John W. Travis and Regina Sara Ryan, Celestial Arts, 2004, www.wellnessworkbook.com.

Quote from *Being Peace*, by Thich Nhat Hanh. Parallax Press, 2005.

Quote from *The Telltale Brain: A Neuroscientist's Quest for What Makes Us Human*, by V. S. Ramachandran. New York: W. W. Norton & Company, 2011.

© 2016 by Cynthia L. Moore
All rights reserved.
ISBN: 0989717003
ISBN 13: 9780989717007
Library of Congress Control Number: 2015906624
The Hygeia Press, Palmyra, VA

To **M**argery Schreiber Payne, my mother, who showed me lifesaving methods of self-care and the deadly cost of unmitigated stress.

And to **A**nnette Fletchall, RD, who, with her humor, easy grace, and presence, put a loving human face on the role of manager.

CONTENTS

Foreword vii
Preface ix
Acknowledgments xi
Chapter I.   Introduction 1
Chapter II. Peace-at-Work Process 11
Chapter III. Ten Simple Skills 15
    1. Minibreak, or "Mini" 16
    2. The EBT Check-In Tool 22
    3. Acceptance: "It's Like This" 30
    4. Yogic Breathing Practices 36
    5. Take a Fifty-Breaths Walk 43
    6. Out of the Box—Shifting Perspective 46
    7. Loving-Kindness, Peace, and Harmony 55
    8. Prayer 60
    9. Claiming Space and Victorious Stance 66
    10. Meditation 74
Chapter IV. Stress and WellBeing: Managing
              Stress Does Matter! 83
Chapter V.   Practice Challenges 103
Chapter VI. Swerving Toward Health: How
              Change Happens 113
Appendix 131
Endnotes and Resources 133
References 137
About the Author 139

FOREWORD

For many of us, the things that shape us in childhood continue to influence our lives in adulthood. At the conclusion of writing this book, I became aware of an old belief, or brain circuit, that was effective and useful in childhood but was no longer the truth or useful for me as an adult.

The circuit "I get my safety and security from being vigilant and in charge," while perfectly adapted to my needs at age six, has caused problems for me as a manager, leader, and mate. Taking charge had its benefits! But I see that this old, once-necessary circuit has also been confusing, heavy handed, and the source of friction in my life. It's been the silent player that has given me a higher level of chronic stress than necessary. Just identifying such an inner pattern can be liberating, and, in this case, it has offered me a new level of freedom. In fact, finding this circuit was like finding the pebble beneath many layers of small discomforts.

You, too, are talented and wise and likely have a great heart full of generosity and wisdom. Yet, even for you, there may be outmoded circuits running you, as this one was running me. In this era, in which neuroscience gives us the cheering news that our thought and behavior patterns are malleable, it's a better time than ever to practice cultivating resilience.

You may be curious about how to find or work with your own circuits. In my experience, life keeps bringing the less effective circuits into view; we can see them in some of the repetitive patterns of our lives. My approach to working with this pattern was primarily to use the self-practice methods of emotional brain training (EBT). Awareness of this circuit came up while I was journaling. Journaling (jotting down thoughts and feelings) has been a valued form of reflection and a supportive companion for me in life. I am using EBT methods to coax this circuit into becoming more pliable for healing and transformation.

You may find that using the EBT check-in or other skills in this book is useful for some of the stress circuits you'd like to interrupt. Practicing any of these skills boosts your secure inner connection and disrupts the automatic responses of old behavioral patterns. It boosts your resilience! When old patterns are causing early damage to our health, disrupting these habitual patterns may be more than a good idea—it may be critical.

Refer to chapter 3 to get started. My experience is that delving deeply into any system of yoga, meditation, or other mind-body practice brings up the old and outdated for renewal and renovation.

May your reading and your journey be blessed. May you know that joy is your birthright. Cheers to enjoying your best self!

With affection and gratitude for our connection,
Cynthia Moore
November 22, 2015

PREFACE

Lest you think this book is a manifesto written by a manager who got it all together and was able to work in sweet harmony with her coworkers while accomplishing great things, let me set the record straight. Early on, one of my coping methods, introduced to me by a food-service manager, was the "scream in the freezer." Method: Open the door to the room-size refrigerator. Walk through the next door into an insulated industrial-size freezer. Close the door. Yell, punch the air, and scream until you've cooled down.

This book represents my journey to learn a wider range of coping skills.

ACKNOWLEDGMENTS

"I have added you to my circle of teachers," a client once informed me. I thought this meant she appreciated our work together. Instead, she explained that, in her tradition of meditation, she would mentally picture her spiritual teachers sitting in a semicircle around her. Before beginning her meditation, she would thank each of the teachers she had assembled. I felt this inclusion in her circle of teachers to be the highest honor—a personal blessing.

With a similar heart of gratitude, I bow to those in my circle. I am grateful for the web of connection with my teachers, many of whom you, too, will meet in this book. I am grateful to those who gave me the tools for my personal stress- and life-management tool kit, and to others who led by example or were faculty at trainings I attended. Even to those challenging people who required that I practice these stress-management skills for my own coping or thriving, I bow in gratitude.

Jane Marinelli, MS, LMT, CHC, was the brave and skillful wellness expert who partnered with me in mind-body skills instruction for clients with diabetes. I was encouraged to take yoga teacher training by Dr. Amrita (Sandra) McLanahan. I am so grateful to Swami Ramananda, who has been the light of Integral Yoga for me as my instructor in basic and stress-management yoga teacher training, as well as a precious advisor and role model; Christopher Leeds, MBA, PhD, for showing me work as play; and Linda Smith, PA, lead instructor at the Duke Integrative Health Coaching training, who inspired me with the security of her inner connection and who taught me the value of shifting perspectives and the methods for accomplishing it.

I have been nourished by the work of seminal thinkers. I particularly appreciate John W. Travis, MD, and his *Wellness Inventory*; Jim Loehr, EdD, for *Toughness Training for Life*; and Laurel Mellin, PhD. I am grateful to Dr. Laurel Mellin for birthing and sharing emotional brain training (EBT) through her books, including *Wired for Joy*, and for the personal and professional development I've experienced as an EBT provider.

I celebrate the many leaders in mind-body medicine who have shown the effects of stress on health and performance. I was fortunate to hear the originator of the term *stress medicine*, Dr. Hans Selye, at a presentation he gave on the effects of euphoric, or positive, stress (he called this *eustress*) and the damaging effects of ongoing helplessness and other forms of what we commonly perceive as deleterious stress. He shared the important fact that what is stressful for one person might be stimulating for another. He gave an example, saying that there are people who, like him, are more like racehorses and others who are more like tortoises, and he said that, while his family members enjoyed relaxing beach time in Florida, vacationing at the beach was a stressor for him.

I am also grateful to Herbert Benson, MD, at the Harvard Mind-Body Institute and Jon Kabat-Zinn, PhD. I appreciate their pioneering efforts in defining the relaxation response, mindfulness, and the benefits of meditation. I feel fortunate

ACKNOWLEDGMENTS

to have studied with both of them via their training for health care professionals.

Swami Satchidananda influenced a tribe of progressive physicians and researchers. I am grateful for the guidance of these leaders, including Dean Ornish, MD. They have been guides for me and for so many others, as yoga science informs modern-day lifestyle medicine. I'm grateful to many teachers at Yogaville and also to Nayaswami Savitri at Sangha/Ananda Village, who have helped me develop what some of my coworkers call "the Zen approach."

My thanks also to the active and retired executives I worked with, who showed me what aging well and victoriously looked like during my time as a registered dietitian and wellness contributor at the Greenbrier Clinic and Resort in West Virginia and Bermuda Village Resort Retirement Center in North Carolina. I also learned, through thirty years of observation as a health care provider in community and teaching hospitals, how stressful patterns of living could contribute to disease development—for example, to diabetes, heart disease, and depression. I feel blessed to have shared an intimate snapshot of life with many clients, often in my roles as registered dietitian/nutritionist or diabetes educator, and more recently as an EBT provider and integrative health coach. To those who have trusted me to partner with them on their healing journey, I am grateful.

Perhaps most importantly, I bow to my inner circle of friends and family. I deeply appreciate these beloveds who helped me birth this book, by offering a steady presence during stressful work events in my life, listening to chapters as I was writing, gently critiquing, and expertly editing. Dear friends and sisters Melissa Pierce, Emily Carsola, Adrienne Jamiel, and Joyce White—thank you for your love and companionship as path partners in this life and also for sharing your creative guidance and your talents! I'm thankful to my friend Wendy Phillips for her skillful editing, and to the team at CreateSpace. Em, thank you for the lovely chapter headings illustrations. I appreciate Sundar Das Ruben Giron, who shared the gift of gorgeous cover photography with me and with each reader.

I feel grateful for my mother, Margery Schreiber Payne, who shared a lifetime of gifts and treasures, as well as a deep understanding of learning from adversity. Thanks to my father, Philip Payne, for his example of authorship in his eighth decade, and my brothers, Andros and Alex Payne, for the inspiring way they are living their lives. I am fortunate to have three other mothers, Helga Payne, Susan Benjamin, and Barbara DeBord, who each affirmed me and the gifts I have to share.

My love and thanks to my husband, Wayland, who adds joy to my life on a daily basis and reminds me with his presence that miracles are possible.

INTRODUCTION

The aim of this book is to help you realize more joy and less stress in your life. It is important to reduce the time and cost to health that it takes to restore balance after extra challenges or stress. Growing your stress resilience skills is the focus, yet the ultimate aim is to enhance joy and wellbeing.

Coping skills work: some more, some less. Some of you will have the same informal stress-management or coping skills I had—like overworking, seeking to be perfect, overeating sweets, spending, and getting lost in movies or romance novels. Others may be more familiar with drinking, eating to numb out or for reward, risk taking, gambling, or engaging in sexual outlets or excessive Internet or TV screen time.

Working too much, with the view that if only I did more I'd get it done and be good enough, hasn't worked so well for me. It's hard to stay balanced at home (enjoying my relationships with my husband and friends while nurturing an active inner life and taking time to exercise, meditate, keep order, and savor healthy foods) when overly consumed by work. My coworkers also communicate their displeasure with my behavior or reactions at times. I can often trace these incidents to my balance having been tipped too far, when I've prioritized getting work accomplished and have lost the ability to relate as my best self.

Over time I've learned some things about how to self-nurture and about my own need for boundaries. I'm learning that nurturing and limit setting are great skills, not only for parenting and personal growth but also in managing people. I continue to find that being a manager is the graduate school of stress management! I think it is even more challenging than finding the sweet spot of healthy harmony in relationships at home.

Few of us intentionally neglect what we know matters to us and to others. Yet the cumulative danger of stress and a sedentary lifestyle can be stealthy and subtle. An active choice may be required to rejuvenate your own health. If you're considering expanding the range of your coping/stress-management skills, why is intervening important to you? Why not continue to feel stressed, get disease, and die early?

INTRODUCTION

We have the power to write a different story than one characterized by self-neglect, disease, and early death. High blood pressure, diabetes, heart disease, depression, and anxiety, as well as some sleep issues, are hallmarks of chronic stress. Disease is more likely to set in when the fight, flight, or freeze stress response gets stuck in the "on" position.

The good news, though, is that whatever our usual patterns, it is possible to interrupt a stress cascade and employ relax-renewal methods. The body's intended match for the adrenalin-charged stress reaction is the relax-rest-renewal response of the parasympathetic nervous system. Studies and clinical experience show that it is actually possible to reverse heart disease and prediabetes. It is also possible to mitigate the effects of depression or anxiety. We can literally rewrite our health story. More peace, along with its benefits, is possible now.

Minimize pain and suffering. It makes sense that, living in a highly stressful environment, we'd distract and soothe ourselves with substances or activities that offer a little, if temporary, relief. (For example, eating sweets triggers dopamine release and a pleasure response in the brain). But as you may have found, these stress relievers have consequences. The consequences of eating sweets as a stress-relieving method may be sluggishness, unintended weight gain, and cardiovascular disease. Many of the consequences actually add to our overall stress and contribute to a host of deleterious life outcomes. See if you recognize some of these for yourself:

Stress-Relief Activity:
Short- and Longer-Term Consequences

Stress-Relief Activity	Effects (Short Term)	Effects (Long Term)
Eating sweets or too much food	Relaxation, calming, sense of reward; triggers dopamine and a pleasure response in the brain	Sluggishness, obesity, diabetes, cardiovascular disease; may alter sleep
Excessive alcohol	Quieting the mind's chatter, relaxation, numbing	Addiction, fatty liver, less ability to respond reliably in relationships, personal safety compromised
Sexual preoccupation	Distraction from other issues or pressure, pleasure response, triggers dopamine, escape from present difficulties	May undermine true intimacy, jeopardizes others or self, legal ramifications
Working in excess or working too hard without breaks or boundaries between needs of self and others	Feeling of accomplishment, financial gain, meeting others' needs, people-pleasing or service, societal acclaim, pleasure response, triggers dopamine	Work-life imbalance, lack of energy for self-care, neglecting own needs, physical or mental health suffering or decline, depletion
Gambling/risk taking	Distraction from other pressures, pleasure/dopamine release	Financial/life chaos, addiction

The real challenge is that we can become habituated to the short-term rewards. Even though initially those rewards may seem innocuous, eventually we need more and more of them to feel the same amount of pleasure in the brain or the same boost of dopamine that these activities used to provide, and they can become destructive. More food, alcohol, shopping, or sex may be required to get the same brain boost. We can get hooked. This increases the likelihood of negative long-term consequences.

More joy, fantastic well-being. The skills of stress resilience that we will be exploring offer ways to interrupt and redirect, bringing us back into balance and a state of healthy relaxation sooner. (Each of us defines balance and thriving according to our own values; we also know when we're feeling our best!) Instead of strengthening our brain circuits of stress and imbalance, we can interrupt a stress reaction and save ourselves from excessive wear and tear on both our minds and bodies. Since joy and pleasure are experienced in the present, this equates to experiencing more joy for the whole of life!

Researchers have identified that stress-resilience skills enhance performance, presence, pleasure, relationships, work productivity, and creativity. In *Toughness Training for Life*, Jim Loehr notes that peak performers and top athletes are able to cycle rapidly between putting out peak energy and engaging in a rest-renewal-relaxation activity. Enhancing your ability to quickly switch into relaxation may help you thrive both personally and professionally. Sounds good, doesn't it?

I have used stress-resilience skills for personal preservation, as well as to manage stress in my work settings. The ten skills that follow are some of the methods that I have found most useful and that I trust you, too, will appreciate. The practice challenges in chapter 5 offer you the opportunity to convert new or remembered skills into reliable habits. I hope you will find at least a few new skills to sample and to add to your personal tool kit. I challenge you to take ten minutes a day to work on these skills, as an investment in yourself.

I worked at the Greenbrier Clinic in West Virginia, an outpatient clinic specializing in executive physical examinations and preventive health care. I'd often ask our clients, "What's your company's greatest asset? Are you caring for that prime asset appropriately?" For many of the executives or business owners, these questions prompted a pause.

If you are that prime asset, either for your company or in your own life, I hope that you won't wait. I hope you will begin to learn and practice these tools immediately.

* * *

Perhaps you're a person who hardly needs this book, because managing projects or other people is not a strain for you. You may be like Hans Selye, a self-described racehorse, who thrives on things that would exhaust others. Yet even if you are not paid to lead others, you are the principal asset in your own life; I expect that these skills will also aid you in your life and relationships.

Becoming a manager may mean leaving behind some of the technical work you initially loved. While taking on a management role may be for the common good or better pay, it may not initially be as innately satisfying as the work you did before. Whether it is in health care, engineering, or military service, the experience of loving the job you trained

INTRODUCTION

to do—and then getting promoted to a position where you seldom get to do the thing you initially loved—can be stressful. Relationships often change when you are part of a leadership or management team. The peer-to-peer camaraderie that is innately soothing for human beings may be harder to access. Both of these stresses are somewhat unique to management. Yet serving as a manager can bring a great sense of triumph, especially if you can learn to manage with a minimum of wear and tear on your life.

I'd like to encourage bringing self-compassion and self-responsibility along on this journey of stress management. We can all find it hard to remember or to practice some of the self-care skills, even those we are convinced have worth and importance. I still need reminders that it's up to me to do this caring for self! I invite you to keep the qualities of kindness, self-compassion, and playfulness close as you expand your skills.

Personal Story

   Last evening I got home at about 11:45 p.m. My workday started at 12:30 p.m., so it was an eleven-hour day. It had been cold working at the office in those last late hours. I felt chained to my desk, doing e-mail. I was chilly and needed a bath. Since I felt sore and tense, I added some Epsom salts as I ran the bathwater. My husband was also coming home late from an event. We each went our separate ways: me to the bath, him to his computer. I said only that I was going to take a bath. I didn't remind him that after an Epsom-salts bath, I'm so relaxed I need to go to bed immediately. So I emerged from the soak—relaxed, feeling exhausted, and so eager for sleep.

What happened next wasn't pretty. I gently announced I needed to go to sleep right away, with the implication for him to respond quickly and depart from the computer immediately—since either option of sleeping in our bed or the guest bedroom involved his cooperation. I readied a bed in the extra bedroom. I again announced I needed to go to sleep right away and kissed him good-night.

He, on the other hand, was chatty. He asked about my schedule for the next day. He wanted me to replace a phone receiver and to share in a technology frustration. Bottom line is that my longing to give in to the delicious feeling of exhaustion by sleeping was delayed just long enough to disrupt my move toward the longed-for sleep. I woke back up, got a second wind, and was not happy. It took a snack of warm milk and reading to calm down and move toward letting go of my attachment to the earlier wave of easy, delicious sleepiness and to the missed opportunity. In the past my tendency would have been not only to get angry but to have a small tantrum. This time I experienced a brief, quietly pissy attitude and expressed my feelings of frustration and disappointment that the talking had caused me to be wakeful instead of allowing the hazy ease of after-bath sleep.

INTRODUCTION

I share this because the next morning I awakened feeling sore. It felt as if I'd done battle with my grumpiness even in my sleep. I also felt sad, guilty, and disconnected from my husband. After my morning meditation hadn't thawed the grumps, I used one of the skills in emotional brain training (EBT). Using the EBT skill, I realized I'd been assuming that it was my husband's fault that I didn't get to do what I had so wanted. I had also expected that he could read my mind. I was acting as if it was someone else's job to do the self-care I needed for my well-being. In my mind, the issue was being tired and not getting the sleep I'd longed for when I wanted it. As I rolled back the page of the day a bit further, I realized I'd worked ten to twelve hours each of the last two days. I'd blown off the personal boundary I'd set for myself to work no more than nine hours a day.

So the takeaway for me, and the more realistic expectation, was that self-care is up to me. I am the only one who can take care of me in such a way that I'm kind to myself. I'm the only one who can know and take care of my basic needs. I am the only one who can leave work after nine hours so I can get home at a reasonable time and have enough time to sleep. I am the only one who can recognize that while I can work with abandon at times, it's not a kindness to me or to others for me to do so. I am the only one who can monitor my needs during the day to set myself up for something other than exhaustion, depletion, and feeling strung out. Self-care is a version of self-love, and it's up to me!

I've had feedback from coworkers that my state of mind and my reactions influence those around me. When I feel calm, it affects the team and the day in our office. When I am feeling stressed, and my reactions tinged with imbalance, the team is likely to be on edge and less productive. I realize that these stressed states occur more when I'm feeling ragged and I'm not allowing myself appropriate self-care. Who wouldn't be more critical and judgmental of others when their basic needs are going unmet day after day? When I'm kind to myself, it's more likely I'll be kind to those who, like my husband or my coworkers, just happen to be around me.

This book is about getting through the moments of stress in life and at work in a more balanced way so that you will be available to experience joy. It contains practical skills you can implement immediately. My hope for you is the same as the hope I hold for myself—namely, that we will take ownership of our own healthy self-care, resulting in kindness toward ourselves and others.

Self-Care Is Up to Me
Prioritizing what really matters may be difficult. Other people's needs often take priority. It's an ongoing part of the journey to learn what we want and need for joy and balance and then to honor that by providing the pauses, boundaries, rest, renewal, and energizing influences required.

II

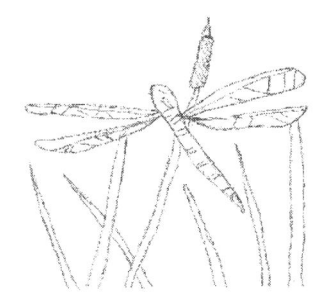

PEACE-AT-WORK PROCESS

Interrupt → Notice → Take Action
In our push-button world, often there is little time to pause and evaluate before reacting. Quick reacting may be premature, for wisdom could come with a few seconds of pausing. Yoga, mindfulness, and other forms of mind-body practice encourage taking time to pause and observe before reacting, for a more effective response. The peace-at-work process puts the pause in operation.

The peace-at-work process involves these three steps:

(1) Interrupting automatic thoughts, activities, or emotions with a pause
(2) Noticing our state of body or mind. Noticing whether or not we need to make an adjustment for either our own benefit or the well-being of those around us.

(3) Taking a self-supporting action. Using a skill to relax and accept or shift perspective. True acceptance is also a form of action.

Several of the *Live, Love, Lead* skills help us recognize and interrupt thought and behavioral patterns and offer a take-notice opportunity. Most of the skills invite greater awareness of the current state in the mind and body. The regular practice of these skills helps condition the brain to internalize peace in our lives, including at those stressful moments.

Stress Management and Resilience—Initial Inventory
As you start on your journey for peace at work and a greater ability to bounce back from stressors, it's good to know where you are now. This inventory may identify what is currently true for you. (Choose all that apply.)

- I don't consciously think I'm stressed but often have physical symptoms that are typically associated with stress (such as a tense neck or cold hands). I wonder if there is something more I should be doing to manage stress.
- I have never thought much about the effects of stress on my health or wellbeing.
- I have attended stress-management workshops or discussions on stress resilience, but I have a hard time putting anything into practice.
- I'm too busy to even begin to consider the issue of stress and how I handle it.

- I am used to things the way things are, and I doubt I can change.
- If I can't do it perfectly, why start?
- I'm very/too aware of the influence of stress on me, though it's hard to make changes or even know where to begin.
- I'm eager to begin practicing these skills, or I have already begun.
- I've been helping myself by getting better sleep, eating well, exercising, or _____.
- I feel like I have a good handle on managing stress, but since there is always room to learn and refine my skills, I'm reading more!
- It seems it shouldn't be so difficult to just do it, and yet I'm not practicing stress management or stress resilience much, and my body is suffering from stress reactions.
- I know how to meditate, and I enjoy yoga when I get there. I feel sorry that I don't prioritize doing these things that could help me more often.

III

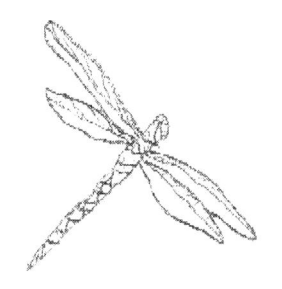

TEN SIMPLE SKILLS

1. Minibreak, or "Mini"
2. The EBT Check-In Tool
3. Acceptance: "It's Like This"
4. Yogic Breathing Practices
5. Take a Fifty-Breaths Walk
6. Out of the Box—Shifting Perspective
7. Loving-Kindness, Peace, and Harmony
8. Prayer
9. Claiming Space and Victorious Stance
10. Meditation

Skill 1. Minibreak, or "Mini"

Definition

Minibreaks can be done as tonics to the irritations of daily life. They often include intentional or deep breathing and help "bring your focus to the present moment, bringing you back home to yourself," again and again. "It's like pressing the pause button," writes Jane Marinelli, MS, LMT, CHC.

Benefits

- They're quick! Can be done in thirty seconds or less
- Reduce stress, inviting calm
- Can be done almost anywhere
- Allow for an intentional interruption in the automatic cascade of thoughts, feelings, and emotions, including difficult emotions or worry

How To

"It is best to insert a minibreak on a planned schedule until you're able to insert them as needed. When stressed, we forget to use or even forget we *have* coping skills that could help," writes Jane Marinelli.

<u>Times to take a minibreak, or "mini"</u>
    Waiting at a red light
    Brushing teeth
    Going to the bathroom
    Before making a phone call or picking up an incoming call

> Before hitting the send button on an e-mail
> Waiting in line
> Getting in or out of a car or similar transitions
> Every time you look at your watch or cell phone
> In the last three minutes of every hour
> When you become aware of feeling tense or stressed

Pairing a minibreak with any routine activity is a way to incorporate these breaks in your life. The following three minirelaxation breaks are useful when dealing with daily hassles. Though simple, they can be extremely powerful.

Option A: Take a deep breath, counting to four as you inhale. Hold the breath for two, three, or four counts. Exhale slowly, extending the exhalation for up to eight counts. Repeat at least once.

Option B: Inhale deeply and hold your breath for several seconds. As you exhale slowly, repeat a phrase or prayer. See the quote below as an example.

> Breathing in, I calm body and mind.
> Breathing out, I smile.
>
> (Thich Nhat Hanh, *Being Peace*)

Option C: Practice belly breathing. Relax the belly and start the in breath by filling the belly. As you continue to inhale, move the air up to fill the middle and upper lungs with breath. Exhale completely. (Exhale air from the upper chest and midchest, and then exhale from the belly). Repeat several times.

About Belly Breathing

When you are first learning belly breathing, it is sometimes easier to learn while lying down. After you get the rhythm of belly breathing, you can do it while sitting or standing and can take it anywhere, from the boardroom to a tension-filled meeting.

If you are practicing belly breathing while lying down, you may want to place a hand on your abdomen. To start the breath, relax the abdomen (belly) and allow it to fill with air; your hand will rise with the belly (frame 1, below). Move that air up to the top of the chest. Exhale completely, letting the hand on your belly come in toward your spine (frame 2, below).

Repeat two to three times.

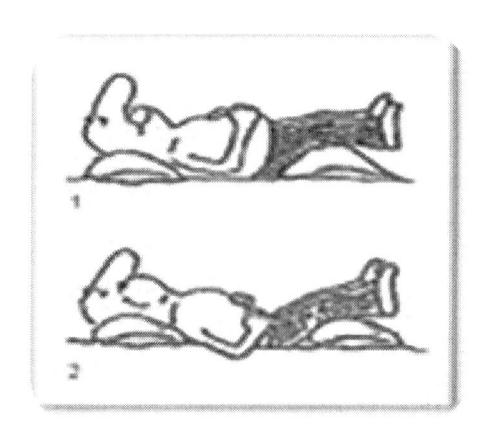

Figure 3.1

Personal Story

Jane always arrived calm and tranquil, like a breath of fresh air, for a late-afternoon class we were coteaching. In contrast, I usually came from a too-busy day of seeing clients. I often felt drained, tired, hungry, a little afraid, and often unprepared. I was frequently worried about details and getting class plans prepared before our attendees descended upon us. You get the picture.

Complicating this was the fact that we were teaching a class series for the first time in which the aim was for participants to learn and practice mind-body skills. Our clients were people dealing with diabetes. We were also conducting research and gathering data each class. We were teaching a variety of mind-body skills, such as guided imagery, journaling, and meditation. I felt the internal pressure of modeling the methods we were instructing participants in while authentically exuding a peaceful persona. I also felt the stress of preparing to lead a class and gather the data appropriately. I wanted to be able to switch from stressed and harried to a state of peaceful calm and centered clarity by the time the participants arrived. Often this was difficult, and I felt only partly successful.

Jane's first instruction to the group was on the topic of "minibreaks"—small things that you can do to interrupt and intervene in the day-to-day stress of life. Of course, you know by now who needed minibreaks the most—me!

I interviewed her one day as we prepared for class. Even though she hadn't been in my stress-laden environment, hadn't she been in some stressful settings before coming in to join me for these classes each week? How was she always able to arrive so calm and tranquil? Here's what I found out: as she walked through the big revolving door at the University of Maryland Medical Center, she would pause to consciously breathe and get centered. She was practicing a minibreak. Jane used the delay of the revolving door to make the transition between the prior events of her day and what was coming next. She used this small transition time as a pause, an opportunity to habitually practice a mini and reconnect with herself.

She coached me over time to explore things I could do as part of my daily routine to find my inner calm. We explored the hazards of my schedule and the lack of time or space to easily find a location where I could get away. My aim became to wind down from the prior activities of the day in the little chapel in the hospital for a few minutes before class time. The plan Jane helped me come up with was for me to take a short walk inside the hospital to the chapel, sit, and breathe for as few as three minutes or use some of the other skills we were teaching. With practice, I did get better.

Today I still use minibreaks. I find that it takes commitment, and even recommitment periodically, to make them happen. I've learned it's easier for me if I link a minibreak or other check-in with another routine activity, like going to the restroom or driving home. Remembering to do them during specific transition times in my day (like during my shower or before a meal) also works. I look forward to the time when these little minivacations become more automatic, as I know they will with practice.

Tips and Pointers
Put a sticky note on your computer or steering wheel as a reminder to take a minibreak. Set your electronic calendar with a code word like "breathe" to remind you. Set an alarm on your phone that can act as a playful reminder to take a minibreak. Change where you wear your watch or Fitbit, and every time you notice yourself looking at the other wrist, practice a smile or a mini.

Skill 2. The EBT Check-In Tool

The EBT check-in is superb when done individually as described below; however, check-ins can be even more rewarding in a group setting.

Definition

The practice of Emotional Brain Training builds stress resilience and promotes healthy balance and greater mental and physical well-being. The EBT check-in is the foundation of the practice of EBT. Use of the check-in and related tools allows you to change the experience of feeling stressed to a more joyful brain/body state more quickly. The EBT check-in, practiced with other EBT skills, is a practical application of the newer findings in positive neuroplasticity, attachment theory, and stress science.

Benefits

- Offers a quick assessment of one's personal state of balance or stress.
- You can use a check-in to know your brain state (relaxed and in balance or stressed).
- You often get a natural feel-good burst of dopamine.
- May result in more positive and powerful feelings.
- May bring clarity about the most beneficial next steps in any endeavor.
- Speeds recovery from a stressful event.
- Gives you far more power to enjoy the moment or to be aware if you're slipping into a stress zone.

- Use of check-ins paired with other EBT tools set you up for peak performance.
- Contributes to a sense of compassion for yourself and for others.

How To

(1) **Belly breathe**. Take a few deep breaths. You may wish to breathe in such a way that your belly moves in and out. Settle into the breath.

(2) **Practice a body position that feels relaxed and balanced**. Make small but important shifts in your posture, such as bringing the shoulders up, back, and down. You may wish to tilt your chin up, bring a smile to your mouth, and invite that smile to travel up to your eyes. Connect inside. This small shift in posture and facial expression (while you are breathing) gives your brain the message that you are in a state of well-being and that you can relax. You can also do a tense-and-relax body scan, starting by squeezing everything on the face up toward the nose and then stretching the face/mouth wide open and sequentially tensing and relaxing all body parts down to the toes.

(3) **Warmly observe**. Warmly observe yourself in the present moment. Observe with kindness and compassion.

(4) **Identify your brain state**. Ask yourself, "What's my brain state number?" to determine your brain state.

Brain State	How You Feel
1	Great
2	Good
3	A Little Stressed
4	Definitely Stressed
5	Stressed Out!

The scaling step of an EBT check-in process allows you to self-assess your brain state—a powerful tool for self-awareness. Just knowing your brain state is amazingly useful.

Accept or Change Your Brain State
Once you've made your self-assessment of your brain state during the scaling step, you are ready to offer yourself one of the following: simple acceptance of your current brain state or the use of the tools to change your brain state.

Simple acceptance of your brain state: "Yes, that's where I am—at 3 (a little stressed); that makes so much sense for how this day has been."
Or
The opportunity to use another EBT tool to change your brain state. The other tools that can help you change your brain state have names like Emotional Housecleaning (brain state 3), Damage Control (brain state 5), and Sanctuary Tool (brain state 1). These tools for each brain state allow you to move

you toward brain state 1. The simple action of checking in and accepting your state may assist you in feeling less stressed.

Tips and Pointers

Using the EBT check-in is a great way to begin to take an active role in reclaiming your well-being. Use it during natural breaks in the day, such as when you wake up in the morning, before or after meals, and when transitioning from one activity to another. You can also set an hourly reminder to do check-ins regularly. It is recommended to do them regularly, ten times per day.

Following your practice of EBT check-ins, please consider enrolling in an eight-week EBT Connect class to learn all five tools.

A caution: If you check in and repeatedly find that you're in brain state 4 or 5, it is best to:

(1) Do check-ins only one to three times a day until you have learned the tools to use in each brain state.
(2) Work with an EBT provider or enroll in an EBT Connect group training class to get supervised instruction on the cycle tool for brain state 4 and the damage control tool for brain state 5. This will allow for more moments at brain states 1 and 2. Practicing the skills for each of the five brain states, including the *stressed* and *very stressed* states, promotes the building of whole-brain capacity and enhances your work, pleasure, and home pursuits.

Emotional Brain Training

Instead of the brain being stuck in stress, which is the cause of 80 percent of health problems, the goal is to move up the brain's emotional set point so that health problems naturally fade and new challenges to health are less likely. An EBT check-in helps interrupt business as usual in your brain and body.

Checking in enables us to pause and reflect on what brain state we are in so that we can see, hear, and feel ourselves and really connect to ourselves. The EBT check-in tool culminates in using the most effective stress tool to return us to a state of low stress and high reward. There are five additional EBT tools, one for each brain state.

The more resilient the brain, the more the brain's habit is to move through stress and back to well-being and joy. Moments of stress provide an opportunity for individuals to become more securely attached to themselves instead of relying on an artificial or addictive substance or activity.

Laurel Mellin, PhD,
November 23, 2013. Author, Wired for Joy.

Personal Story

I have been a provider/trainer of EBT for more than ten years. Why? Quite simply, I found the tools in this system to be extremely powerful in my own life. It's also a thrill to get to share the check-in and related tools in EBT with others. Often EBT class participants note that they're amazed at the traction they can get on previously very difficult things in their lives. That has been my personal experience also.

I found the first book on this method in the late 1990s. It was called The Solution. The book, written by Laurel Mellin, was about weight management, and it had the word "permanent" in the subtitle. I was impressed by the mind-body approach and pursued training to become a certified provider. (It was called the solution method then and later revised and renamed emotional brain training). I really thought the training would just be a formality and that I already had the knowledge and skills. I begrudged the necessity of so much time and personal work in the EBT workbooks/training kits. Little did I know the personal benefits I'd receive!

As I did the experiential personal work and academic training to be able to teach the skills to others, I found that my own intimacy skills and interpersonal limit setting and boundary skills really improved. The solution method/EBT gave me the skills to know and express my feelings and needs better. As a result, I felt safe enough in a relationship to decide to marry for the first time, in midlife. I credit EBT training with my happy marriage. The check-in and other skills also came in handy during the power struggles of early married life!

The early origins as a method of weight management changed to what is today called emotional brain training and EBT Connect. The early method showed benefits in areas other than just improved health and weight. It became clear that EBT skills, including the check-in, were a public health application of some of the newer findings in neuroplasticity.

What is my practice like today? Check-ins often are going on in the background of my life, like a beneficial, well-practiced habit. One characteristic of my best days is that I've done six to ten intentional check-ins. I'm more receptive to seeing and savoring delight and joy on those days. However, in patches when stress mounts and balance in life is more precarious, I can still get caught up and forget to offer myself a full check-in. For me, in times of higher stress, it's often about just remembering to check in. Sometimes it's also about the willingness to take the time to do each of the brief steps that I know makes for better balance for me. Even though I know that checking in feels nurturing and I'll feel more whole afterward, sometimes my task-oriented drive to push on, despite accelerating stress, competes with my willingness to pause and check in. Even being present with all of the emotions (including the negative emotions I may experience during a check-in) is actually nurturing and useful. It still takes effort, however, especially when I'm stressed. Often when I'm stressed is when I most need the check-in!

I'm fortunate to facilitate classes in EBT several times a week. In each class session, we do a group check-in. I love the relaxation and reset that I experience after a luxurious, slow group check-in. I encourage you to use one or more EBT check-ins as a brief vacation during your day!

Many people benefit greatly from taking the initial eight-week EBT Connect training to learn the skills to use for each brain state. Classes are held in small groups, facilitated by a certified EBT provider. These small-group settings allow for learning as a community via social emotional brain-to-brain transmission with real-time practice.

Skill 3. Acceptance: "It's Like This"

I was introduced to this practice by Dr. Jeff Brantley, a psychiatrist and mindfulness teacher at Duke Integrative Medicine in Durham, North Carolina. After leading us in some breath-awareness mindfulness, he invited us to notice the thoughts in the mind, to notice feelings, and to just accept that whatever we noticed was, for now, "like this." He invited us to allow nonjudgmental awareness; to be with the breath. This invitation to accept things as they are rather than to strive or want to make them different had the effect for me of curbing the usual chatter and analysis of my thinking mind. "It's like this" gave me a sweet taste of mindfulness.

> The skill of "it's like this," with its implied acceptance of things as they are in the moment, serves to fortify my personal value of operating with an open heart as often as possible at work and at home. There is recognition in mindfulness teachings, and in yoga practice, that we are not our thoughts and we are not our responses. When events arise—whether internal or external—repeating the phrase "it's like this" creates a pause, a moment that allows for choosing to accept things as they are. Repeating "it's like this" also gives us a moment to recognize any judgment and to let go of it. It creates a small space of possibility for viewing the circumstance as it is versus as we might like it to be or as we expect it to be.

Definition

"It's like this" includes the mindfulness principle of letting go of judgment. One of my colleagues defines "it's like this" as "an empowered relationship with the facts on the ground."

Benefits

- Can be used in any setting
- Is an active form of letting go of judgment about internal responses to external events
- Helps us to be present with physical or emotional pain
- Reduces frustration

How To

- Breathe. Invite yourself to be present in the moment. Notice what is present without trying to change it. You may notice the feeling of sensing the chair beneath you or the feeling of the air on your skin. You may notice the feeling of your breath or the feeling of your body. Bring your attention to the thoughts. Notice the automatic nature of thoughts.
- Use the phrase "it's like this" internally in response to thoughts, emotions, or other sensations that arise in the mind or body.
- Continue breathing, and while allowing things to arise in the mind, simply repeat, "It's like this."

- Notice any allowing or acceptance of things as they are. Soften or relax your body, belly, chest, and shoulders.

Tips and Pointers
The way I practice "it's like this" is almost as though I am letting go of something I'd been holding on to. Often I take a few breaths and notice body tension that indicates that I've been grabbing for or expecting a specific outcome. By contrast, silently stating to myself "t's like this" while doing my best to accept that this is the way things are—at least for now—feels like a relief. With this internal shift, I can let my shoulders and my body relax. Especially in times when I feel at the mercy of something unpleasant, stating "it's like this" is a step I can take that allows me to shift into being present and feeling curious. The process of letting go to see how things are allows me to be more present and to notice what is available instead of what I want, what I am expecting, or what I am judging.

For example, my training is as a registered dietitian/nutritionist, and I get to work with clients, teaching them EBT. I am also a manager. It is hard for me to have a silent inner tantrum in my managerial role without the judgmental part of me rearing its head and saying, "Oh, yes, and I see you've really got these stress-resilience EBT skills down; where are they now?" Using the perspective shift that "it's like this" helps me to rapidly and effectively sidestep the personal judgment and self-criticism that arises in these times. I am able to see myself with open eyes, a little humor, and some self-compassion through the lens of "it's like this."

"It's like this" also quiets my judging mind about people or circumstances that I wish were different. It's a portable tool that can be helpful while waiting in line at the grocery store, when working to meet a deadline, when engaging in a frustrating employee interaction, or when feeling captive in a nonproductive meeting. For me, saying "it's like this" to myself replaces judgment with patience and acceptance. It allows me to observe things just as they are, without trying to will them to be different. This skill helps me breathe deeper, relax my belly, and let my shoulders down. I suspect that it eases lines of tension in my face. My experience is that it's much easier to smile and relax with "it's like this" playing in the background of my mind. It's almost like a private joke or the replay of a pleasant experience in its capacity to act as a warm companion at stressful times. Since this practice allows me to relax internally, I notice that it also helps me to feel more comfortable and safe in my own skin.

Personal Story

"It's like this" served me well on a recent family trip. My brother took me with his family to a remote camping area on a grassy slope high above the Monterey Peninsula in California. What a beautiful high hillside seat we had for watching the sunset over the Pacific!

After the cookout and before we prepared for sleep, the winds started and the temperature dropped. I am a light sleeper at the best of times. I realized that only those sleeping in the truck were likely to get much sleep, while those of us in tents would have a long, wide-awake night. Using "it's like this" helped me stay present to savor this adventure and the beauty of the night. As hour after hour of the chilly night passed, I enjoyed the starry sky through the flapping window on my little tent. Though I slept little as the wind howled, "it's like this" helped me to be able to enjoy the experience of camping rather than worry about how little sleep I was getting.

"It's like this" is my favorite process for being present in the moment. This simple phrase keeps me from judging myself, others, or situations, when I remember to use it. It allows me to be present with things as they are.

―⸺

Mind-body researcher John Astin, PhD, shared with me the following seven foundations of mindfulness practice. They are based on both ancient tradition and the work of Jon Kabat-Zinn, PhD. The practice of mindfulness is like cultivating a garden. A garden flourishes when certain conditions are present. Holding these seven qualities in mind, reflecting upon them, and cultivating them according to our best understanding will nourish, support, and strengthen our ability to be mindful in every situation.

- Nonjudging: to observe simply and impartially. To experience something without clinging, judging, or wanting to push it away.

- Patience: accepting the spaciousness and power of a hopeful stance. Allowing time for things to unfold.
- Beginner's mind (also often called "Zen mind"): being willing to look at things from the view of an infant who is experiencing something for the first time (rather than through the lens of our usual patterns or judging mind).
- Trust as self-reliance: trusting the place of strength, goodness, and wisdom within and that it's possible to listen and honor our own inner truth/authenticity.
- Nonstriving: opening to notice our own usual patterns of reaching to attain things. Instead of grasping to achieve and reach, simply observing and being present with what is. Nonstriving can be a great tonic that allows one to simply be present.
- Acceptance: seeing things as they are right now and allowing them to be as they are rather than how we'd like them to be or think they "should" be. Acceptance follows from nonstriving.
- Letting go: involves all of the other six qualities. Letting go represents the allowing of things to be as they are, move change, recognizing that all things do change.

For me, using the phrase "it's like this" incorporates the foundational qualities of nonjudging, patience, nonstriving, acceptance, and letting go. "It's like this" allows for being in the present moment while expericncing an easing of judgment.

Skill 4. Yogic Breathing Practices

Definition
Breathing practices are called *pranayama* in the yoga tradition, and they are one of the eight elements of the yoga system for health. *Prana* means breath. Breathing practices are often the first step toward inner balance.

Three-part breath is also called "complete breath." This powerful pranayama practice starts with exhaling completely to empty air from the lungs; then inhaling into the belly area, moving the breath up to the midchest and upper chest; and then slowly exhaling from the upper chest to the lower part of the lungs. The three-part breath is an important stand-alone yoga breathing skill. It is also used at the end of a rapid-abdominal-breathing series. The three-part breath is a safe and effective way to tap into the significant power of yogic breathing, even for beginners.

Rapid abdominal breathing is a yoga practice of forceful exhalation. The yoga term for this breath, *kapalabhati*, means "breath that clears the mind and emotions." Like other yoga and breathing practices, rapid abdominal breathing works with subtle energies in the spine to clear some of the subtle energy centers in the brain. This practice includes a vigorous series of exhalations followed by a complete exhale and a deep three-part breath.

⸺⸻

Personal Story
Rapid abdominal breathing was introduced to me by someone in a leadership position at one of the

major yoga institutes in the United States. He noted that rapid abdominal breathing was what he used when he needed to manage anger or dispel negative emotions quickly. This individual had the challenge of demonstrating yogic conduct in addition to the usual ideals of managerial restraint and steadiness under pressure. When I heard that this yoga-breathing skill was useful for him, I was curious and later convinced. He reported that when he could feel the intensity of anger or another big emotion clouding his judgment, he'd do two or three quick rounds of rapid abdominal breathing before returning to the task, person, or management issue at hand.

I've used rapid abdominal breathing when there was nothing else to do. I recall a stressful interaction when my anger was rising exponentially. I didn't feel safe to continue talking effectively in an employee interaction. I excused myself, found a private spot, and started this powerful breathing practice. Just two or three minutes of this practice allowed me to calm down. I felt more peaceful and more balanced. I was able to return to the interaction with what felt like a small, yet important, buffer zone.

Benefits

- Oxygenates blood, enhances alertness
- Exercises the diaphragm
- Can neutralize strong emotions

- Clears the mind
- Can improve sinus and allergy problems
- Stimulates digestive organs
- Energizes
- Sets the stage for calmness

How To: Three-part or Complete Breath
Bring your attention to your breath. Without changing anything, take a few moments to observe how you normally breathe. Notice whether it's mostly in the chest or in the belly area or whether both places move when you breathe.

Lie down to get this next sensation. Place one hand on your chest and the other on your abdomen (see diagram under section on minis, 3.1).

To start or learn the inhale:

-Exhale completely by bringing the hand on the abdomen toward your spine. Also let all the air out of your chest. Completely exhale.
-Begin your inhalation by expanding your abdomen. Fill the abdomen with air first, allowing the hand placed on it to rise as you breathe into the abdomen.
-Gradually move the air up your chest. Fill your rib cage and then go all the way up to your collarbone area.

To exhale:

-End the breath with a slow, steady exhalation from the top of the chest, the middle of the chest, and, last of all, the belly.
-Bring the belly in toward the backbone to fully exhale.

You may want to practice another three-part breath just so you see how it makes you feel. Return to breathing normally.

This is a beneficial stand-alone core yoga practice. In the beginning you may feel complete by practicing the three-part breath. If you would like to try something more challenging, you can proceed with rapid abdominal breathing (instructions below).

How To: Rapid Exhalation
This breathing practice looks as if you are snapping in your abdomen while blowing a bit of fuzz out from your nostrils. After five to ten rapid nasal exhales, you exhale completely, leading to a long, slow three-part breath.

To start, blow your nose if you are congested.

- Place a hand on your stomach/abdomen, and say "ha, ha, ha" out loud while snapping your abdomen in forcefully. Notice how your stomach area moves in the middle of your belly as you say "ha, ha" vigorously. Pause.
- Next, close your lips, and pretend you're blowing fuzz out of your nose. Push air out of the nose with some force on the exhale so you feel it leaving your nose.
- Put the two together:
    - Instead of saying "ha, ha" out loud, keep the abdominal contractions as though you were saying "ha, ha," but close your mouth and breathe out through your nose, as if exhaling a bit of fluff or fuzz.

- Blow the "fluff" out the nose five to ten times. Without consciously taking in another breath, your body will automatically backfill the breath.

Great! By now you've probably got the basic rapid abdominal breathing moves! Pause.

Putting it all together for rapid abdominal breathing:

- Become aware of the normal breath.
- Take a breath in and do five to ten rapid exhalations, snapping in the abdomen on your exhale while blowing out from the nose.
- Exhale forcefully and completely.
- Start the three-part breath by inhaling deeply and then exhaling deeply.
- Return to your normal breathing pattern.

Often in yoga settings, you are invited to do a round of five to ten rapid abdominal breaths. This is followed seamlessly by a complete exhale, a three-part breath (deep inhale, deep exhale), and then a short period of normal breathing. This process can be repeated for a total of three rounds.

Tips and Pointers

It is best to practice rapid abdominal breathing on a mostly empty stomach. Do not try to do this after a big meal.

Like many of the skills in this book, rapid abdominal breathing is best practiced ahead of the time you need it so that it's available as an automatic resource in a time of higher stress.

You can do the three-part breath sitting, standing, or lying down. I think it's easier to learn the three-part breath when lying down, since you can picture a wave coming into your abdomen and filling the chest and then the upper chest, and you can feel or see the tide ebbing as the breath empties from the upper and middle chest and then finally from the abdomen. Once you are familiar with the three-part breath, you can sit in a chair or on the floor in a cross-legged position. You are usually sitting to do the rapid abdominal breathing.

Many yoga teachers can spot you or check your technique if you would like to ensure that you're doing this breathing practice effectively and safely. Integral yoga is the tradition I'm trained in and that I most closely endorse. Many yoga traditions offer a version of rapid abdominal breathing, or *kapalabhati*. Your best bet is to find a certified yoga instructor in the integral-yoga tradition.

A word of caution: In some settings I've seen this practice done to an extreme (so many repetitions that it feels dangerous to me, at least for those who are just beginning). As with any yoga or breathing practice, listen to your own body/experience and modify instructions to suit your personal needs and preferences. Trust your body as the authority. Breathing practices alter the energy in the body and mind. As with weight lifting or getting in shape to run a marathon, where regular training with lighter weights and moderate distances is better than undertaking an extreme practice too quickly, so it is with yoga breathing.

Practicing the three-part, or complete, breath at the end of rapid abdominal breathing restores balance to the right and left hemispheres of the brain, which means we are better equipped to most effectively manage whatever situations occur.

The practice of three-part breathing and rapid abdominal breathing also helps the diaphragm muscle stay in shape. (Hearty laughter is another great way to move and strengthen the diaphragm!)

Skill 5. Take a Fifty-Breaths Walk

In addition to the benefits to the mind, the fifty-breaths walk can bring balance back to the body, serving to rebalance and ground our energy.

During the fifty-breaths walk, pay attention to your breathing, in and out, as you walk. Depending on your pace, the walk takes about six minutes. Consciously breathing fifty times while walking also serves as a mantra or focus for the mind. What I love about the fifty-breaths walk is that I get the mind-body benefits of both walking and breathing!

> The Fifty-Breaths Walk relieves the eye tension that builds up from extended periods looking at a computer screen or something at a close distance. The muscles of the inner eye may tighten, and the eyes may lose their elasticity and ability to focus on near objects. I have noticed that when I am away from my computer screen for extended periods, like when I am traveling, my eyesight improves dramatically. Now I find that taking a break to focus on distant objects, especially by going for a short walk, is a great way to keep my eyes relaxed and my vision in good shape.
>
> (Swami Ramananda), *Integral Yoga Institute*

Definition
A walk outside that includes counting each breath during walking. Each complete breath cycle (inhale and exhale) counts as one breath. This practice continues until you reach fifty. If you lose your count, start over.

Benefits

- Helps you become aware of the present moment.
- Improves clarity and presence for the concerns of the day.
- Can become a walking meditation.
- Walking increases brain-derived neurotrophic factor (BDNF). BDNF plays a role in memory and learning.
- May shift your perspective to greater positivity.
- Gives your vision a rest from screen time and gives you a break from too much sitting or a hunched posture.
- It is heart healthful if you extend the walk.
- Reduces sedentary/sitting time.
- Improves blood pressure and blood glucose through walking and stress reduction.
- Aids in weight management, especially if combined with other movement during the day.
- Increases the *prana* (life-force energy) available to you through walking and breathing in fresh air.

How To

- Walk outside.
- Count your breaths as you walk (each complete inhale and exhale counts as one).
- If you start thinking about the past or future and lose count, return to counting the breaths.
- Conclude the walk after fifty breaths, or extend the five- to six-minute walk to ten or fifteen minutes to get the other health and brain benefits from walking.

Tips and Pointers

It is easy to let your mind wander and forget to count the breaths. When this happens, just note that your mind has wandered. Restart the counting until you can get fifty consecutive breaths while walking. It's fine to count with your fingers.

Skill 6. Out of the Box—Shifting Perspective

Definition

Perspectives are points of view. Examining an issue of concern from other perspectives can help us get unstuck when the current views are limiting. Reframing is another method for taking a different perspective. Many things help us to shift perspectives: media, music, inspirational movies or reading material, the influence of friends. This playful practice invites you to intentionally experiment with varied perspectives.

Benefits

Shifting perspective generates one or more new vantage points with new possibilities. It can also positively affect interpersonal relationships, including those with your employees or family. Perspective play allows exploration of other possible vantage points and can enhance creativity. Widening one's perspective may change or improve decision making.

How To

There are many ways to play with shifting perspective. One example:

- Define the issue you wish to examine from other perspectives.
- Draw a circle in the middle of a piece of paper and around it draw petals as though you were drawing a large daisy flower. This is your form for this exercise. (There is also a sample form in the appendix.)

- Write the name of the issue you would like to examine—for example, *annual reviews at work*—in the middle of the flower. Give a name to the perspective or view you currently hold on this issue *(Evaluations are a chore)*. Place that on one of the petals.
- Identify other possible perspectives. Give these perspectives names. Feel free to be creative, emotional, or whimsical: *waste of time, time for connection, the perspective my dog would have on this issue, blight on my life*, and place each of these possible perspectives on a petal.

If you get stuck, you can always pick "view from above/mountaintop view/small airplane" as an option; taking an aerial view will almost always shift the perspective. Recently I realized that "hot air balloon perspective" was a new favorite.

Something that can feel overwhelming in day-to-day life may look less daunting or important from the distant perspective of a small aircraft. If you're needing levity, add the perspective of your pet, an oak tree, or your favorite movie character to one of the petals.

- For each perspective, ask yourself some questions:
  1. If this perspective had a color, what would it be?
  2. How would I feel (or how would my body feel) if I adopted this perspective?
  3. What would be possible in this perspective?
  4. Do I want to move toward or away from this?

Pick one or two perspectives that seem possible or most appealing. Imagine that you are responding to the pending issue from this perspective. See if this opens up new options or approaches. A blank form is located in the appendix.

One of the initial responses to stress for humans is a pinpoint-clear mental awareness. It's as though, in response to the stressor, our perception is sharpened and our thinking is hyperalert. If the stressful situation continues, however, instead of heightened clarity, the range of options eventually narrows. We see fewer options and may be missing opportunities. Using the perspectives approach as a stress-management skill allows us to add play, lighten up, and view the situation from angles other than our own. Playing with perspectives is another way to widen the view. Looking at a problem from varied perspectives can be a form of brainstorming; it may contribute to an expanded range of potential solutions.

Personal Story

The results of an integrative-health-history questionnaire I took rated my stress level as rather high. I suspected that the managerial parts of my job were what stood between me and optimal health. I realized I'd been expecting myself to be responsible for others at work. Given my origins as the oldest child in a single-parent household, taking care of everybody brought up some old emotional patterns for me! As I did the following perspectives exercise, I realized how little I liked this being-responsible-for-others management perspective. In that perspective I felt shut down (not excited, stale, unenthusiastic, dutiful, and even resentful).

So I named some other possible perspectives to experiment with ("holistic manager," "fun at work," "ideal manager," "just a job," "I am responsible to myself and others"). The last option seemed and felt the best to me, though "fun at work" has also been appealing.

After filling out my shifting perspectives form, I felt unusually tired. Since I was at home and had the opportunity, I took a nap. During the nap, I dreamed that there was a frog inside the house. It was away from its natural outdoor terrain. It had apparently been inside the house for some time. It still could move weakly to get away if prodded, but its jumping capability was nearly gone. In the dream I could tell the frog was getting tired and worn out. Relocating the frog outside felt like an urgent matter, since the time indoors seemed life threatening for it. In the dream I was deliberating about how to capture it (without too much touching) so I could take it outside. I was considering where to take it, where there would be shelter and also moisture, when I woke up.

I added "frog out of water" to my perspective petals. Even without looking at the color, body feel, or questioning what's possible in this perspective, I recognized its truth: I am a frog out of my ideal element in my current managerial role. I have survived a good while in this environment. But like the frog in my dream, it's time to relocate or adjust for health and well-being. Exploring what is possible from this perspective may include really considering what my best habitat is.

Having the dream helped me realize a perspective for both the short term—I am responsible to myself and others—and also the long term. From the perspective of the frog out of water, I can see the longer view and the likely path for future decisions.

In the dream, the body feel of fear seemed to be a message to me not to gloss over or wait too long to realize the parallel to my own life. How long have I been "indoors" and out of my element? What is my ideal element? Will I power on and override this perspective? I suspect in this case, the *Frog out of water* perspective has given me a sense of urgency. I wonder what a *Frog in water* perspective would be like? Would I have had this dream or understood its meaning if I hadn't been exploring different perspectives?

Figure 3.2 Perspectives Step 1: Define the issue.

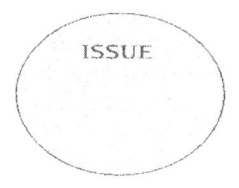

ISSUE

TEN SIMPLE SKILLS

Figure 3.3 Blank perspective form. Step 2: Use the form to identify five ways you could see this issue. Give those perspectives names.

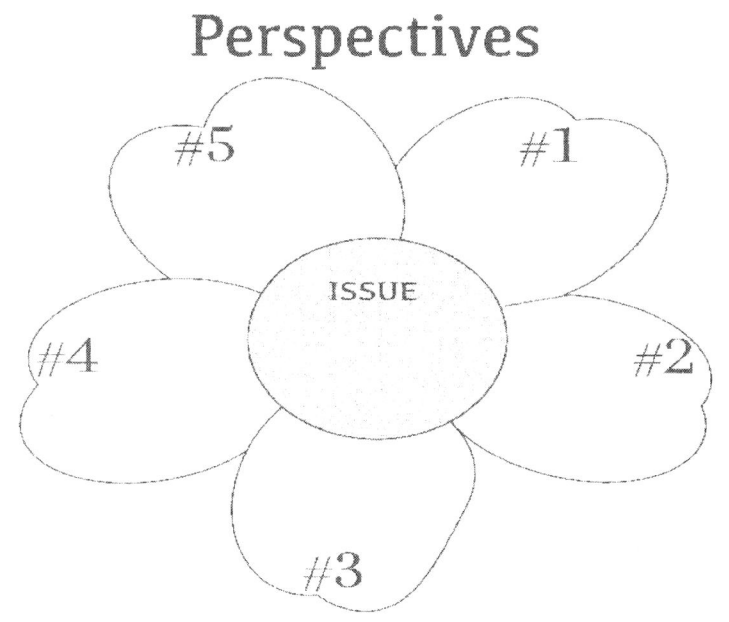

Perspectives

#5 #1
#4 ISSUE #2
#3

1-5 Possible perspectives or vantage points for dealing with the issue

What are some of the ways you could view this issue? List three to five possible perspectives.

Steps:
(1) Name/define the issue.
(2) Identify several possible real or fanciful perspectives.

LIVE, LOVE, LEAD

(3) Explore each possible perspective via the questions below.

Questions to ask of/in each perspective
 If this perspective had a color, what would it be?
 How do I feel in this perspective?
 What would be possible in this perspective?
 Do I want to move toward or away from this?

Figure 3.4. Example of a perspectives exercise.

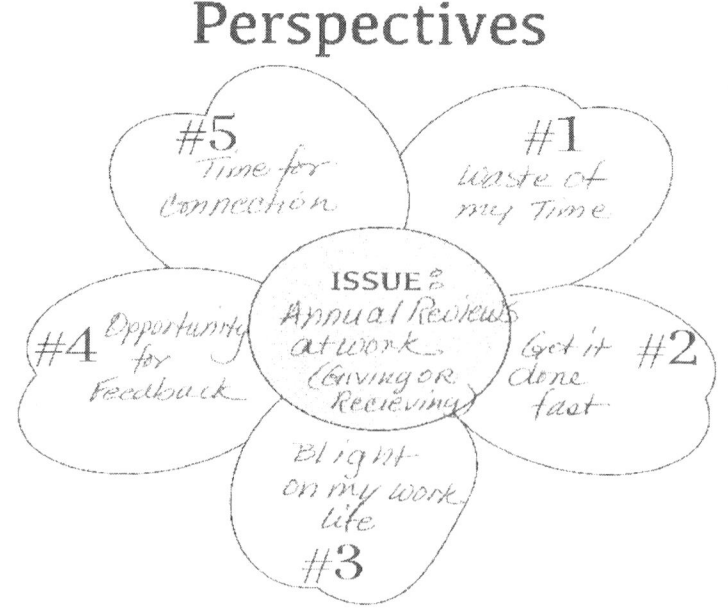

Perspectives

#5 Time for Connection

#1 Waste of my Time

ISSUE: Annual Reviews at work (Giving or Recieving)

#4 Opportunity for Feedback

#2 Get it done fast

#3 Blight on my work life

1-5 Possible perspectives or vantage points for dealing with the issue

52

Outcome: you may be able to look at the issue from some varied standpoints by using the perspective worksheet. It may not change the basic issue, but it may allow you some new approaches or ways of viewing the possible ways to work with the issue. You may even find an approach you'd never considered. In my experience, it can defuse indignant energy and allow me to see things from another person's vantage point.

Perspective work can tap into the power of the creative right brain. The following notes from my journal are an example of this creative brain process.

Personal story

I'm newly married for the first time, in my fifties, and dealing with the somewhat predictable power struggles in the new-to-me relationship of marriage. My frustration with various concerns at work continues, as do a stack of other stressors. A friend and yoga luminary, Swami Ramananda, suggested I read *Peace Is Every Step* by Thich Nhat Hanh. He suggested once and then twice. After more of my stories, requests for help, and probably some whining, he suggested *Peace Is Every Step* again. Somewhere along the line, I purchased the book.

I was at work the first time I opened it with the intent to read. I was delighted by "Tangerine Meditation." Another time, it was "The Dandelion Has My Smile." I was in. Both brief readings helped me feel the beauty of being in the moment. They helped shift my disposition and my perspective. Each reading brought me back to my heart and my own sunny disposition. This is the original book on being at peace. I now have those colored, clear 3M page-marker stickers on many of the pages. Reading a page is part of my lunch routine when I have a personal minute. Each brief story helps me shift my perspective and adopt a more positive view.

Asking myself "Are there other possible perspectives?" when I get stuck in a management trench has offered me some new insights. I've playfully tried on the perspective of whimsical things—the perspective of my cat, a stately tree, a favorite movie, a Greek god or goddess, a character in a book I admire, or a favorite flower—as sample ways to look at something from a different point of view. Sometimes playing with perspectives reminds me that the most available options (like my own view and other entrenched perspectives) aren't the only ones. Just like the brief readings in *Peace Is Every Step*, some small change in my point of view can help me operate from a different, more enjoyable perspective.

Skill 7. Loving-Kindness, Peace, and Harmony

Definition

One of the presents I received from mindfulness-meditation training was being introduced to the loving-kindness meditation. It's a way that mindfulness and compassion can be extended into the community. Sharon Salszburg, author of *Lovingkindness: The Revolutionary Art of Happiness*, gave me the teaching that stuck. The instruction was to practice loving-kindness meditation with the self, a beloved, a neutral person, and then a difficult person. I've found the loving-kindness meditation to be very helpful in management settings, as well as in personal relationships. It is a practice rooted in Buddhism, and the specific wording changes in various traditions.

Benefits

- Opens the heart to feelings of wellbeing for the self and others.
- No limitations to who can be the recipient or how often it can be used.
- Restores a sense of internal clarity.
- Practiced regularly, it transforms relationships, moving them toward greater harmony.

How To

Often the loving-kindness practice may follow a period of quiet or brief meditation. Begin by sitting quietly and taking a few breaths. Repeat the following with genuine care and clear intention.

Repeat for yourself:

> May I be safe.
> May I be happy.
> May I be healthy.
> May I be peaceful.
> May I live a life of ease.

Repeat for another person:

> May you be safe.
> May you be happy.
> May you be healthy.
> May you be peaceful.
> May you live a life of ease.

Personal Story

I wasn't excited to be going to work. A coworker I had challenges with was coming back to work. The coworker's vacation time away had been a vacation for me too! I'd enjoyed the respite from conflict, and I was dreading the idea of having to interact again. I wasn't looking forward to Monday. I considered what might be useful. Was there a tool in my stress-management practices that could help? I settled on doing the loving-kindness blessing for myself and for this individual. I practiced the loving-kindness blessing or meditation outlined above for a couple of days.

By Monday I felt as though I'd straightened out the energetic clump of crossed wires between us. I felt somehow protected and better able to keep my heart open to the possibilities of feeling connection with this individual. My prior sense of being mired in fear and anticipation of difficult outcomes had diminished. It did help. It was a harmonious day.

Since then, I have found this loving-kindness practice to be a steady ally.

Several years before, I'd taken a day-trip to Yogaville, home of Integral Yoga in Virginia, just to put some work pressures in perspective. I thought of it as a kind of emergency-room trip to experience some measure of peace. Although I was a random day visitor, I noticed that the noon-group meditators that day were absolutely peaceful. I was curious as to why. What I found was that Sharon Salzburg was offering the featured program that weekend. I was permitted to join for the afternoon, and the loving-kindness meditation was among the things she taught us. I had plenty of raw material to practice with! She sent us outside to walk and practice "May I be safe, may I be happy, may I be healthy, may I be peaceful, may I live a life of ease… May you be…" I firmly locked in this powerful skill, along with the winter trees, January sky, and soaring birds. "May I be safe, may I be happy, may I be healthy, may I be peaceful…"

When I came back to work after that weekend, I was so at peace within and even felt at ease with the difficult person at work! I noticed a significant uptick in my compassion. I also started using it with my husband and began to notice that many of our rough edges at home also straightened out.

I suspect that the simplicity of this instruction helped me remember it, even though, in my own practice, I've changed the order of some of the wording. In case her specific guidance is as powerful for you as it was for me, here you have her instruction, reprinted, of course, with her blessing.

> May I be safe.
> May I be happy.
> May I be healthy.
> May I be peaceful.
> May I live a life of ease.
>
> (Sharon Salzberg, *Lovingkindness*)

Another version of loving-kindness that I use in this phase of my life includes slightly different wording. I am grateful to mindfulness instructor Susan Stone for this version.

May I be happy.
May I be healthy.
May I be peaceful.
May I be free from inner and outer danger.
May I live a life of ease.

Practicing either version of loving-kindness meditation is likely to be very fruitful. Regular practice may also benefit your relationships at home, at work, and in your social or spiritual community.

Skill 8. Prayer

Definition

Since prayer is so individual and personal, I'll just offer a few thoughts from others.

> Prayer—cry of the heart. (Tami Simon, founder of Sounds True)

> [Prayer is to] stop and think; focus. Generally it helps to have my eyes closed so I'm not distracted. Usually occurs after I've done something stupid in the car: a lot of my prayer is "Thanks!" (Wayland Moore)

> Prayer is:
> 1. an act, practice, or an instance of praying; entreaty; earnest request; 2. the offering of adoration, confession, supplication, thanksgiving, etc., to God or a god; 3. the form of words used in praying; a formula of supplication, esp. one addressed to God. (*Webster's Dictionary*, 5th ed.)

> Gardens can be as unruly as a field of wildflowers or as ordered as a bed of neatly planted flowers and shrubs. Prayer, like a garden, can be loose and free, or formal and structured. Some prayers are shouts of joy, while others are cries for comfort. We sometimes dance when we pray; other times we simply breathe and enter the silence. (*Daily Word*, October 27, 2013)

This verse from Matthew was one of my grandmother Jean Robertson Schreiber's favorite scriptures. Grandma's interpretation was that when two or more agree and the Divine is also present, as in a group prayer, that prayer is strengthened.

> For where two or three have gathered together in My name, I am there in their midst. (Matthew 18:20)

Benefits
The benefits of prayer are determined individually. Here are some that I experience:

Calm: A sense of calm when I've uttered or requested a prayer. I feel better when I've communicated my hope or concern and have handed it over in a prayerful way. Silent Unity is a prayer ministry located in the Midwest that prays with the caller and then submits the prayer request to others who offer prayer for the next thirty days. I call Silent Unity with prayer requests when I'm worried about family members or friends. Have I used prayer and made requests to Silent Unity for the insurmountable challenges at work? You bet. I've also made prayer requests for my clients, patients, and coworkers. Knowing that prayer will continue for thirty days is a comfort and a relief.

Harmonizing: When my husband and I got married, I proposed that we say a form of grace before our meals together. The grace might be to hold hands and have a quiet thank-you. I notice a difference in our connection and harmony when we've been able to have at least one daily grace together versus when we've been traveling and eating in settings where this quiet minute of hand-holding under the table isn't feasible.

Even the body takes a cue from this simple act of thanksgiving and harmonizing. Studies show that the body digests and assimilates food suboptimally under the influence of stress. Taking just a few moments to experience gratitude or offer another form of prayer is enough to send signals of relaxation to the brain. Pausing, breathing, and connecting with yourself or another is enough to allow your body's digestive machinery and insulin levels to respond in a way that is more supportive of optimum health.

Relief: It feels wonderful to just let go and stop a worry cycle through prayer!

Positivity: The work of Barbara Fredrickson, PhD, at the University of North Carolina, Chapel Hill, shows that a three to one positivity ratio is the healthy combination (three positive thoughts to one negative). The more positive thoughts a person has per day, the healthier and more enjoyable his or her life is likely to be. For me, prayer and positive affirmation confer big benefits.

Changing brain patterns and health: Many spiritual, healing, and meditation traditions include word and sound vibrations that produce beneficial resonance. Some of these benefits have been witnessed via changes in functional brain scans.

Benefits include improved mood and reduced depression and anxiety.

What do you notice about your quiet prayers or hopes of your heart?

How To
I believe that talking with what I sometimes call the inner presence or with God-as-nature is an innate human capacity. Opening the inner dialogue does not need to be taught. Limiting screen time or creating nonscreen quiet time, however, may need to be practiced! Listening within or inviting silence/space via journaling are reliable ways to invite an intimate lifelong communication.

> Keep me as the apple of the eye, hide me under the shadow of thy wings."
>
> (Psalm 17:8)

Personal Story
I've heard it said that prayer is talking to God and meditation is listening to God. For me prayer is closely tied to the longings of my heart. My God has become a friend and a beloved presence. The Divine is often with me—in my consciously calling out, as well as in my unconscious longings and inner

hopes. My experience is that these longings can actually be prayers.

I used to go in the summer to Omega Institute in upstate New York. Sometimes I'd fly in from the Midwest or southern states. Other times I'd take the train. Often I'd have a brief stop in Rhinebeck, New York—just long enough to catch the shuttle bus to Omega. Each time I'd look longingly at the Beekman Arms, an impressive old hotel in town. My wish was more of a longing than a prayer; I at least wanted to take a look inside. Each time, there would not be enough time to go take a quick peek before I'd need to be at the shuttle pickup.

Years later, when I'd been hired at a five-star spa resort in West Virginia, the Greenbrier, I was sent to Hyde Park, New York, for a weeklong training at the Culinary Institute of America. Some of the chefs invited me to an after-hours presentation and dinner. After a long car ride, imagine my delight and surprise when we arrived at our destination, and it was the Beekman Arms Inn in Rhinebeck! Rather than a mere peek inside, I was treated to an elegant dinner.

So for me prayers are intimate. Who else could have known this small but deep longing in my heart? How else could this random wish have been met and surpassed?

Prayer for me is a sense of the Divine presence that is eager to move my longings into manifestation. It teaches me that being conscious of my longings may be the loudest prayer of all.

The words of others, via sacred texts, music, lyrics, and so forth, can also become prayers. These often function for me as thought stoppers. A thought stopper can be a prayer, a hymn, a line of scripture, or a phrase said as a substitute for worrisome thoughts. Training through *A Course in Miracles* includes a process of undoing old assumptions. An example of a thought stopper I use, paraphrased from *A Course in Miracles*, is "I do not know what anything, including this, means, and I will not choose to let the light of my own past learning guide me now." This helps me pause.

This passage reminds me to recognize that my perceptions and ways of viewing may not be the only right way or the accurate light with which to view a situation in front of me in the present. I unhand my absolute assumptions and let some other glimmers of possibility in for consideration.

> I do not know what anything, including this, means.
> And I do not know how to respond to it.
> And I will not use my own past learning as the light to guide me now.
>
> T-14.XI.6:7-9 *A Course in Miracles*,
> Foundation for Inner Peace

Skill 9. Claiming Space and Victorious Stance

Definition

Claiming space and victorious stance are physical movements that can shift personal or group vitality quickly. These activities lift the mood and can be beneficial as a conference break. Both energize by moving breath in the body. Claiming space is energetic and playful; it can be a fun way to discharge tension in a group or private office setting. Victorious stance offers relaxation to the head, neck, and shoulders and sets up a body stance of joyful expectancy. When victorious stance is done quickly, it's a way to prepare oneself for successful interaction and to consolidate personal power. An alternate name for victorious stance is victorious heart pose.

Benefits: Claiming Space

- Moves energy from stuck to playful
- Oxygenates the body and mind, increasing alertness
- Can be used as an icebreaker, conference break, or between sedentary activities
- Discharges negative energy

TEN SIMPLE SKILLS

How To: Claiming Space

(1) Begin in neutral stance, with knees slightly bent.

Figure 3.5 Claiming space starting pose. Stand relaxed, with slightly flexed knees.

(2) Exhale on a "ha!" sound while extending your right arm diagonally down (forty-five degrees) to the right, palm open and facing downward as you sidestep the right foot to the right.

(3) Inhale while returning the right arm and leg to a neutral stance.
(4) Exhale on a "ha!" sound while extending your left arm diagonally down (forty-five degrees) to the left, palm open and facing downward as you sidestep the left foot to the left.

TEN SIMPLE SKILLS

Figure 3.6 Claiming space—in motion
Step left, extending the arm forcefully, using a forceful verbal "ha."
Step back to center.
Stepping right, extend the arm, verbally express "ha!"
Repeat on each side for several rounds.

(5) Inhale while returning to a neutral stance.

Continue for three to five rounds or until you're feeling energized. Stop if you feel dizzy.

Personal Story

I was preparing to lead an experiential EBT class. It's desirable for the leader to be in a highly balanced brain state since the class is about stress resilience. Right before class a coworker sent me several frustrating e-mails, basically insisting that I take action on certain details. I was deep in my managerial responsibilities and far from a balanced brain state. Since the class was about to start, I needed to shift quickly to being present with an open heart and a clear mind.

When the members of this small EBT class assembled, I told them I was still deep in managerial stress. I wondered and asked if they wanted to learn a method for physically shifting their body state quickly.

When they agreed, we walked to an open area in an adjacent room, so we'd have some space for this activity. I demonstrated claiming space: the stance of standing and saying "ha!" while taking a step to the right with the outbreath and then back to center and repeating on the left. I encouraged breathing in on the center stance, then out again on the right, breathing in on the center, and out with a forcible "ha!" as the arm went way out to the left. The group seemed startled at first and then intrigued. They joined me, and we got louder and more powerful, swinging and punching our arms out to the right and left while shouting "ha!" It took only five repetitions on each side before we were all energized and smiling.

The coworker who had so recently triggered my stressful feelings walked into the room right at this time! Usually I would have felt an internal contraction, a shrinking feeling, and a desire to get away. Instead, I noticed that the smile on my face was genuine, fueled by the body state of balance. In just in ten breaths while doing claiming space, I had, in fact, been able to claim my space. I'd shifted from frustrated to a playful state of unshakable balance.

Our little troupe said that they really enjoyed the claiming space exercise. The beauty of this practice is that you can do it as though it were a martial art. You can practice with a more or less forceful "ha!" You still retain the power as long as you step forcefully to each side and extend your arm with the outbreath. It's also a way to add play—a known stress reliever!

Please try claiming space in your own life settings! I was delighted to hear that one of the brilliant engineers in my own family used this with his creative partner in their work setting just prior to a Silicon Valley meeting. He found that it reduced them to giggles and lightened the meeting atmosphere. Still another family member used it as a pretest ritual to combat test-taking anxiety. I just find it fun and energizing to do in a workshop setting.

Victorious Heart Pose

Part of this movement originated from stretches in *Yoga for Stress Relief* by Swami Shivapremananda.

Benefits: Victorious Stance

- Relaxes tension in the upper back, neck, and shoulders
- Allows for a much deeper breath, especially when done somewhat slowly
- Energizes if done quickly
- Is likely to boost mood and create a sense of joy

How To: Victorious Stance

This movement can be done sitting or standing, so it's perfectly adapted to an office or conference setting.

(1) On an inhalation, look up while lifting the arms up into a wide V shape.

(2) Exhale through an open mouth as you stretch your arms out in front of you to shoulder height with your palms together facing each other and far enough apart to hold a beach ball. Allow the upper back to round slightly while looking down.

(3) Repeat steps one and two, continuing for three to five rounds or until you're feeling energized and relaxed.

(4) To close the position: from the V shape, exhale as you bring your hands down palms together in front of your heart/chest.

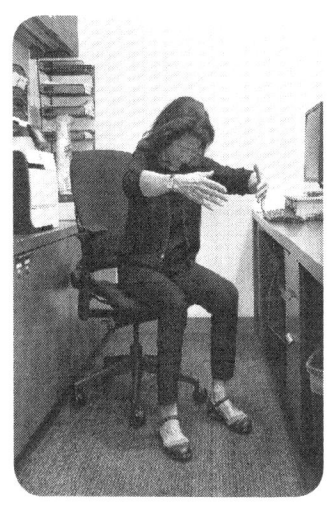

Figure 3.7. Victorious heart pose, reaching forward.

Figure 3.8. Victorious heart pose, V shape.

Skill 10. Meditation

Definition
Meditation has been described as listening to the Divine, or listening to the quiet presence within. Meditation often includes adopting a focus for concentration or reflection. It can be done sitting, as it is often depicted, but also when walking and in other positions. The Ananda Center teaches that meditation has two parts: getting there and being there—that is, practicing preparatory techniques to calm the body and breath, which lead to a deeper meditative state. Both parts can be called meditation. Mindfulness meditation also teaches that all stages of the experience are part of the meditation.

Mindfulness meditation, mantra meditation, and yoga nidra types of meditation all confer benefits to the individual meditation practitioner. Many forms of meditation provide societal benefits also. Even contemplative prayer belongs here, as it invites listening.

Mindfulness meditation is the practice of focusing attention on one's breathing and internal bodily sensations. Often a kind/compassionate observation of thoughts, feelings, or body states is included in mindful awareness or mindful meditation. Yoga nidra has sometimes been called "yogic rest," and, in the integral yoga tradition, it is the concluding part of a yoga class that helps align the individual with his or her own blissful nature. Mantra meditation lets a word, sound, phrase, thought, movement, or object be the focus for the mind during meditation. A cardiologist and an early pioneer in meditation research, Herbert Benson, MD, identified these features shared by many forms of meditation he studied:

- Focusing on a thought/word/object/motion as a point of concentration
- Repeating that focus of concentration (thought/word/object/motion)
- Bringing the mind back to that focus when it wanders

While there are many types of meditation—some secular, some spiritual—I appreciate the simplicity of this description from Dr. Benson.

Benefits

- Interrupts the stress cascade of emotion and thought
- Promotes a healthier steady state in the body
- Lowers blood pressure
- Decreases heart rate
- Changes oxygen consumption beneficially, similar to sleep
- May lower stress hormones (cortisol, epinephrine/adrenaline) or reduce the time these stress hormones circulate
- Restores balance more quickly
- Confers benefits to immune function
- Improves mood

Benefits of continued regular practice of meditation:

- Decreases chronic psychological distress
- Improves markers of aging, such as telomere length (telomeres cap the ends of DNA, and longer telomeres have been associated with longevity)

Boston College researchers found that the present-moment focus enabled by mindfulness meditation improves well-being by allowing individuals to become aware of sensations, emotions, and thoughts that arise in the mind with less judgment or reactivity. Mindfulness meditation allows for a wakeful alertness that enhances vitality.

Benefits of meditation for leaders:

- Allows you to return to the present moment, where you can make better decisions
- Improves focus
- Puts things in a larger perspective, allowing you to step back
- Can restore empathy/kindness for yourself, others, or the situation
- Supports your growth as a manager

How To
Meditation can be done in any position (sitting, standing, or walking) and in varied locations (at home, at work, or in the car). Sitting meditation is often preferred since it's one way to build a meditation habit with fewer distractions. Getting the body calm and comfortable but energized will help with meditation practice.

Preparation—Sitting Meditation
It's best to sit so the spine is straight.

You can sit in a chair where your hips and your feet are supported and you are sitting tall with an upright spine. If you prefer to sit cross-legged on the floor, it can be more comfortable to sit on a cushion or folded blanket.

Part of the preparation for a successful meditation is to activate your energy before meditation. You can do this by taking several deep breaths or doing a body scan.

To accomplish a body scan, alternately tense and relax your body from head to toes. You can start by tensing and then relaxing your face; tensing your right arm and fist, and then relaxing; tensing your left arm and fist, and then relaxing; tensing your buttocks, and then relaxing; tensing your right leg and foot, and then relaxing; and tensing your left leg and foot, and then relaxing.

If you know your body is tense or you're feeling anxious, you can also prepare for meditation by taking a short walk or doing a few yoga stretches.

These steps of first finding a comfortable sitting position and activating your energy are useful for quieting the mind in preparation for the active portion of meditation.

Active Meditation
Choose a focus for meditation.

The focus can be on your breathing and the feel of the breath coming in and going out of your nostrils or your body. The focus can be on a word or words; it can also be an image of something, such as a flame or flower, or just listening to the sound of the breath. Sometimes pairing the breath with words is useful.

In this example we'll use breath and words: Focus on being aware of the breath. As you breathe in quietly, say the words "I am." As you breathe out, say the word "home." Repeat breathing, saying "I am" as you inhale and "home" as you exhale. You can say this audibly and eventually quietly. Using the inhalation, say "I am," and on the exhalation, "home."

- Allow yourself to become still.
- Concentrate on what you've chosen to be your focus.
- When the mind wanders, gently but firmly bring it back to your chosen focus of concentration.

Stay with this practice a little while; even if your mind wanders, just bring it gently back, even if it stays only a few moments longer. Even seconds of peace are beneficial!

Example: Imagine that, instead of meditating, you were preparing a meal. You've just prepared a marvelous meal and now are sitting down to enjoy it. Imagine the ingredients, the preparation, the aroma. Rather than eating quickly just to satisfy hunger, imagine taking time to savor the meal. Imagine taking time to enjoy the beauty of the ingredients and dishes, even if it's simple fare. Take an extra few moments to enjoy the abundance of beauty and flavor, savoring each small bite.

Consider the same strategy with meditation. Give yourself the pleasure of a few more breaths, a little more time to savor the peace of meditation.

Closing the Meditation

> Now that your mind is calm and steady, you have the opportunity to give yourself a little gratitude for having taken the time to quiet your mind. Know that by this simple act of concentrating and

meditating, you are remapping your brain's neural circuitry in favor of more balanced responses. You are feathering the nest for a soft landing the next time you're stressed. You are building your cave of inner peace, a few meditative breaths at a time. Appreciate that!

> Observe how the breath, and thus the mind, slows down and naturally moves into short pauses; these pauses are the times when peace truly pervades one's breath, body and mind; it's a very joyful feeling! Enjoy those peace-filled moments and "string them together" until you not only become inwardly peaceful, but you can feel that you have become Peace itself.
> —*Nayaswami Savitri*
> *Ananda Sangha/Ananda Village*

Practice becomes firmly grounded when well attended to for a long time, without break and in all earnestness. (Sri Swami Satchidananda, *The Yoga Sutras of Patanjali*, sutra 14)

Personal Story

Meditating in the morning is essential for me. I need the morning meditation for balance and to be the person I aim to be.

Even though I'd been introduced to meditation as a child, I realized how essential meditation was in my life during graduate school. The requirements for a master of science degree in nutrition at the University of California at Davis seemed a big stretch for me, both academically and financially. I felt out of my league compared to my peers and the expectations of the faculty. In addition, I was offered a teaching-assistant position, which helped with tuition costs but also added to my workload. I soon realized that if I didn't prioritize morning yoga exercises and meditation, I'd be in trouble, as I'd be unable to keep up with the intensity of being a teaching assistant while also having student responsibilities.

Even though time was extremely limited, meditation became nonnegotiable. It made a significant and measurable difference for me in this high-intensity situation. What I learned was that, especially when I'm too busy, and time is limited, and life feels overwhelming, it is even more important to meditate than when life is easy and smooth.

Tips and Pointers
Being comfortable physically in meditation is important.

- If you are sitting on the floor to meditate, it can help to put one or more pillows under your hips so that your pelvis is tipped slightly forward and

you don't need to engage your abdominal muscles much to sit upright.
- If you are lying down to meditate, it's best to have something warm and comfortable underneath you: a cushioned mat, carpet, towel, or cotton blanket. You may find you can relax more easily if you put a bolster or rolled-up blanket under your knees. Alternatively, placing the soles of your feet on the floor about hip-width apart and letting your knees fall together can support relaxation in the low back area. Meditation is most effective when done in a sitting position, with the spine upright. Lying down to meditate is the best option only if you are unable to sit up due to physical limitations or are practicing a yoga nidra type of meditation.
- The best time to meditate is whenever you will do it. Often mornings are preferred, just after you have awakened. Morning meditation also gives you a gentle start and buffer for the whole day.
- Meditating is best on a mostly empty stomach. Before breakfast or dinner are popular times.
- Build your success with meditation by having a community with whom you can practice similar skills.
- Some things that can bring ease and benefit to your meditations include having a dedicated spot at home or in the office, meditating at a regular time of day, using a wool or silk rug, carpet, or cloth under the place where you sit, and having some kind of a ritual prayer, scripture, or candle to initiate your meditation at home.

Meditating regularly helps build a strong, steady practice. Meditating frequently gives you an inner core of peacefulness and tranquility.

* * *

But his delight is in the law of the Lord and in his Law doth he meditate day and night. And he shall be like a tree planted by the rivers of water that bring forth his fruit in his season; his leaf also shall not wither; whatsoever he does shall prosper.

(Psalms 1:2–3)

* * *

Meditating is like diving into a clear deep lake.

(Amrita (Sandra) McLanahan, MD)

IV

STRESS AND WELLBEING: MANAGING STRESS DOES MATTER!

Let's put stress and the lack of true personal peace into context. The human stress response is the high-alert feedback system that coordinates action in the mind and body. Its aim is to get us out of danger when we're in trouble. It's important to recognize that this system is designed to keep us safe. However, sometimes our stress-response system can get stuck and can react to all input around us as "life or death" situations, affecting our health and the health of those around us.

When stressors surround us and we don't have the opportunity to slow things down, discharge stress, and return ourselves to balance, our body, brain, memory, and concentration all take a hit. When the body is on high alert and the stress response is flipped on, the blood pressure, heart rate, blood sugar, and blood fats all may get elevated, since they are part of the mechanism preparing us for fight or flight. This coordinated cocktail, released during stressful times, seeks to give us the fuel and endurance to run or to fight a predator.

In dogs and other animals, the corresponding body stance is called "shackling": a puffed-up chest, hairs standing on end, and muscles taut. This is how dogs prepare to pounce, fight, or flee. In humans, if a stress reaction is prolonged, it can result in our own form of shackling. Humans are more likely to experience this as a tension in the neck and shoulders, chronic pain, tense facial muscles, anxiety, and eventually an increase in health care visits. Unmitigated, stressors may take their toll in the form of headaches, low back problems, and mood changes like anxiety and depression. There is a personal, health, economic, and business cost to chronic stress. Left unchecked, stress also can—and does—damage our relationships.

Responses to Stress
Humans respond to stressors in three key ways: physically, mentally, and behaviorally.

STRESS AND WELLBEING: MANAGING STRESS DOES MATTER!

Physical	Mental	Behavioral
Initial short-term response		
Tight neck and shoulders	Hyperalert	Fight, flee, or freeze
Blood pressure rises	Acute vision	Relationship conflict
Blood fats go up (cholesterol, triglycerides)		
Elevated blood sugar	Anger	
Protracted stress		
High blood pressure	Poor concentration	Procrastinating
High blood sugar/prediabetes	Irritability	Hiding/distancing/raging
	Depression	Excessive use of alcohol/food Spending in excess
Eventually		
Heart disease, diabetes	Impaired memory	Addiction

Clearly we're at our best when we can limit our stress response to short-term episodes and then cycle back into balance quickly. When we are able to do this, we have more of ourselves available for personal pleasure and to share with others. A prolonged stress response may set us up for poor performance both at work and at home and may predispose us to addiction, impaired intimacy, and disease.

Oscillation Promotes Balance
Humans are wired for contrast. Many things in nature have cycles and seasons. Our natural patterns are a dynamic cycling between expending energy via work, study, play, or movement, followed by rest, renewal, or restorative time. Benjamin Franklin remarked wisely on this balance of satisfying work and rejuvenating rest.

> Early to bed and early to rise,
> makes a man healthy, wealthy, and wise.
>
> (Benjamin Franklin)

This quote is a call to wake early and, at the same time, an encouragement to get enough rest. It notes the importance of the cycle of wake and sleep for outcomes of balance and meeting his measure of success: to be "healthy, wealthy, and wise."

We are more likely to be out of balance when we don't have the contrast of satisfying work or energy output alternating with times of rest, relaxation, celebration, or play. Some believe that lack of sufficient contrast is a setup for stress to take its toll, creating a spectrum of symptoms, including burnout, depression, anxiety, and other imbalances. Burnout is an example of outputting too much energy over a long period of time without relief and can result from a prolonged stress response. Depression may result from insufficient stimulation or a lack of satisfying engagement in life or work.

Jim Loehr, PhD, has coached athletes and performers toward excellence and peak performance by encouraging natural movement or oscillation between a stimulating amount of energy expenditure (or modest stress) and rest and recovery. He developed methods to put people in the ideal performance state (IPS). He uses the image of a wave to indicate energy output and the lull between the waves (rest and renewal) as an effective way to demonstrate the importance of cycling between these two states.

Loehr, along with another brilliant leader in health care, John W. Travis, MD, MPH, capitalized on the work of Nobel Laureate Ilya Prigogine and his discovery about how molecules communicate when they're moving in waves or oscillating. Others, like Dr. Irving Dardik, have hypothesized that even our immune system functions below par without a healthy balance between energy output and rest, as in with excessive stress or too much relaxation.

In the IPS, Dr. Loehr notes that positive feelings such as calmness, relaxation, confidence, and joy predominate and that there is often a sense of fun and fulfillment. In *Toughness Training for Life*, elaborating on the theme of the essential nature of oscillating waves of contrasting experience, Dr. Loehr hypothesizes that there is peril if we don't find ways to have these contrasts in our lives. "If you don't create waves naturally, your body will find a way to get your chemistry moving—possibly by the use of killer drugs such as nicotine, cocaine…or the abusive overuse of caffeine, alcohol or food." If we don't find healthy natural ways to oscillate, to live balanced lives—"the response our body forces on us is very likely to be destructive or even tragic." So the relevance here for leadership and stress management is that we need a balance of work or other high-energy pursuits and also restorative practices, such as sleep, rest, touch, play, or time in nature.

Dr. Loehr likens excessive energy output or too much stress to overtraining in sports, which can lead to a prolonged stress response and burnout. He compares a lifestyle of too little challenge (insufficient energy expenditure or stimulation, or too much rest and renewal) to undertraining in sports. Peak performance is achieved by cycling between high output and rest and renewal several times during every day.

Figure 4.1. Stress and recovery in balance.

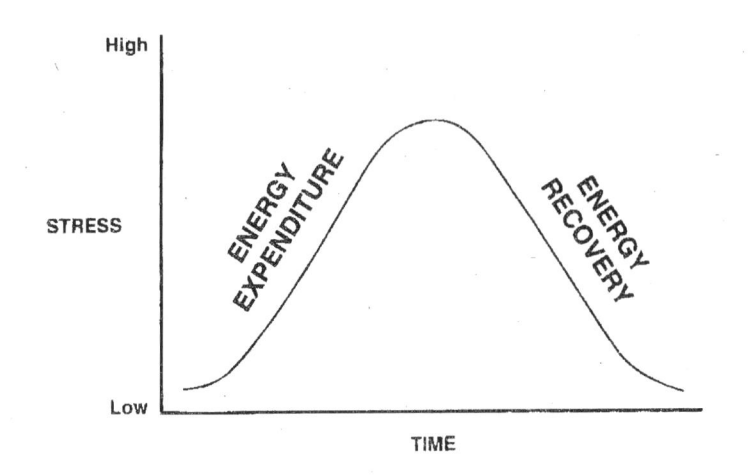

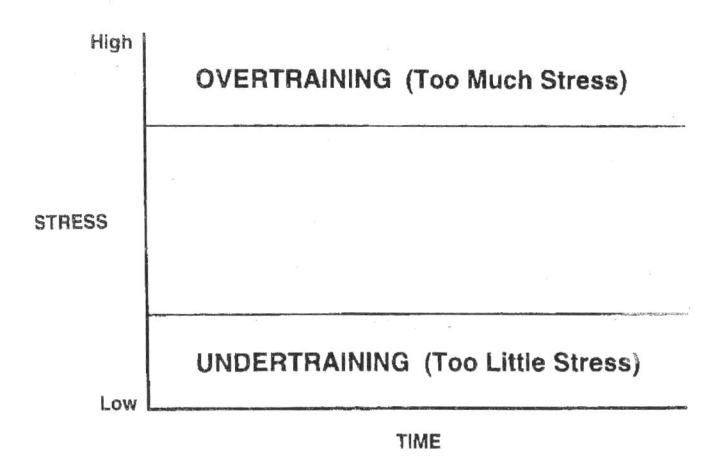

Figure 4.2. The continuum of stress.

```
High |
     |   OVERTRAINING (Too Much Stress)
     |  ─────────────────────────────────
     |
STRESS
     |
     |  ─────────────────────────────────
     |   UNDERTRAINING (Too Little Stress)
Low  |_____
            TIME
```

Personal Story

The ancients knew about the benefit of contrast. For my fortieth birthday, I went to Greece. I felt excited the day we got to go to Epidaurus—one of the ancient outdoor theaters renowned for its acoustics. As a sidelight, the tour guide showed us the remains of a healing temple, the equivalent to an early hospital. This "hospital," or temple of the Greek father of medicine, Aesculapius, was within a short walk of the fourth-century theater. The guide noted that viewing both comedy and tragedy (contrasting, emotionally laden performances) was often part of the therapeutic prescription for the sick in ancient times. So during a healing stay at an

Aesculapian hospital, rest, sleep, and taking the waters would have been routine. Exposure to intense contrasting emotions (via the theater) was also apparently part of the "cure."

Adaptive Stress Is a Balance of Energy Output and Relaxation
Adaptive stress is the process of taking in and responding to changing conditions in a way that strengthens the organism. When stressors exceed our ability to remain balanced, mind-body wear and tear can mount. As leaders or managers, we plan and project, meter our time, and budget resources, but the unpredictability of the management environment introduces threats and changes we cannot predict. It's important to recognize unpredictability as an actual stressor and to keep our stress-management skills well honed for a rapid return to peace and balance.

The instinctual mammalian response to fear, danger, and threat are to "fight, flee, or freeze." These responses don't work so well in our modern world because our modern-day dangers aren't what they once were; we seldom need to escape being some creature's dinner!

Today's stressors come in subtle guises, but they can be cumulative and damaging. Running from a predatory animal: such a good idea and a highly effective strategy as long as we manage to escape. Running to escape a stressful coworker or fighting via e-mail at the office day after day: not practical solutions to modern stressors. Sick days, mental-health days, and disability may represent our modern-day attempts to run or escape.

STRESS AND WELLBEING: MANAGING STRESS DOES MATTER!

Although primitive responses get automatically triggered, we may not discharge the threat physically, thus increasing our overall health risk. The stress hormones that induced high blood pressure, high blood sugar, and high blood fats don't get utilized. They just sit there, predisposing the body to physical diseases. The intrapsychic pressure or threat may also persist and may be damaging to our physical or mental health. The hostility research by Redford Williams, PhD, and colleagues shows that a quickness to anger can predispose individuals to early heart disease. People who walk, run, or move for exercise thus really do discharge tension and help their bodies return to balance.

Too often, many of us shortchange time for rest and renewal. Sleep, exercise, eating, and satisfying connections with other humans are primal needs. These activities help restore balance and switch the internal stress response from on to off. Switching into rest and renewal mode more often during the day decreases our stress load and fosters health and balance. When we're too busy with high-output bursts of energy, or when our stress meter gets stuck in the on position, it often leads to burnout and can contribute to premature disease.

> Apart from breathing, satisfying thirst, and eating, sleep clearly is the most important recovery activity in our lives. It is also the body's largest circadian rhythm. Disruptions of this critical recovery rhythm can have serious health and performance consequences.
>
> (Jim Loehr, EdD,
> *Toughness Training for Life*)

Figure 4.3. Burnout profile (visual).

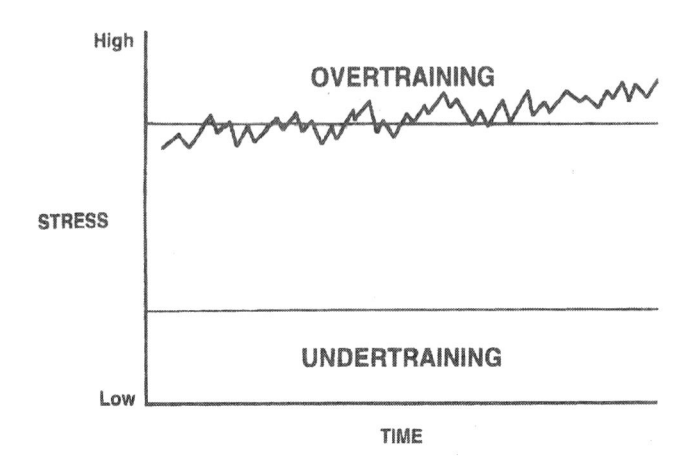

Figure 4.4. Depression profile (visual).

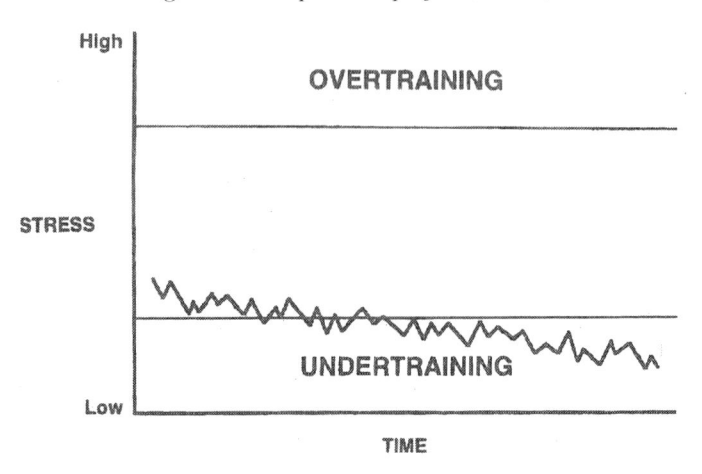

In both states of burnout (overstressed) and depression (less stimulation than needed), the necessary wavelike motion, or oscillation, of output and renewal does not occur appropriately.

> One way to nip a stress response is to identify what we need for more contrast or oscillation in our lives.

Reflection Questions:

- What would my personal profile look like?
- What do I need in order to feel even more satisfaction with my work, service, or volunteer activities?
- Am I spending enough time in relaxation? Too much? Using healthful means to relax or relying on substances or activities that jeopardize my well-being?
- Do I need to find new ways to savor, relax, and play?

How Our Stress Influences Others

From physics and neuroscience to spirituality and health, the evidence is accumulating that what we are thinking and feeling privately is transmitted to others around us.

- Physics research tells us that subatomic particles relate to each other within the small unit of an atom. Apparently it is possible to put a spin on an electron on one side of the atom, and electrons at the other side of the atom react in concert with the electron that has been altered. There is communication, or a relationship, at the level of subatomic particles. Should we doubt, then, that this communication is taking place within our own bodies?

- Mirror neurons are evidence that when something active or emotionally relevant occurs with someone we're watching, there is a corresponding response in the neurons of our own brains. Mirror neurons are brain "cells that are active during a movement and while watching another perform the same movement," James W. Kalat writes in *Biological Psychology*. According to neuroscientist V. S. Ramachandran in *The Telltale Brain*, mirror neurons "lie at the heart of our ability to adopt each other's point of view and empathize with one another."

Personal Story

This was an experience from many years ago in Texas. My friend took me to a workshop. One aspect of this event made a big impression on me. The leader asked the assembled group of about twenty to twenty-five people to identify and contemplate our most negative qualities and to keep them in mind for the next few minutes. She took time out to whisper something in one man's ear and then went back to leading the imagery for the group. She invited us to get quiet and focus and dwell on our own most negative, ugly, dysfunctional qualities.

My initial experience was of seeing my selfishness, and I began to replay my ugliest, gut-sick, unforgiven behaviors with my mother and others—in short, to begin a heart-heavy slog through what was horrible or off in my human dealings. Very soon, however, I began to experience a sense of understanding the soup out of which those ugly attributes had developed. I began to feel a real sense of loving compassion for myself—a tenderness toward myself. I felt sad that these dysfunctional means developed within me, but also a real sense of love for myself and an ease—in short, a self-forgiveness. After this self-love and compassion began to come up, I kept trying to be the "good student" and to return to the assignment—to bring up another negative quality and to dwell on it. I was simply unable to follow the original directions. Before the five- to eight-minute imagery period ended, I felt stronger inside, aware of a feeling of love and inner connection I had not felt before. Rather than feeling worse about myself like I'd anticipated when the experience began, I felt peaceful and self-loving.

At the conclusion of the group practice, the leader asked a few people to share their experience. Three or four people did, and their experience was like mine. They each had also started with the laundry list of their ugly traits but soon found it difficult to dwell on their negative qualities. They related that they'd come to a place of experiencing warmth and kindness to themselves.

The leader then revealed what she'd whispered in the ear of the one man. She'd asked him to do something different than the guidance given to the rest of us. She said that she'd asked him to link up to the "I am" consciousness, the spirit within himself that felt connected to the Divine. She'd asked him to maintain that connection during the guided imagery, or during the time she was instructing the other twenty to twenty-five of us to hold on to and dwell on our most negative qualities.

So although the "I am" consciousness was new terminology to me, I understood that what this one person was doing had seemingly influenced the rest of us in a way that was remarkable. Because he'd been doing something linked to a different and apparently powerful energy, the group had not been able to dwell in negativity. Since I had my own felt experience and then heard my experience echoed by others, this felt real. Although I'm not a scientist, this did have the feel of a small scientific experiment for me.

The takeaway for me was that one person can have a powerful effect on others by staying in positivity and peaceful connection.

* * *

Twenty years later, on 9/11, I watched with bewilderment and fear as the Twin Towers collapsed. I traveled back from Annapolis, Maryland, that day to my home in Baltimore. The next morning I knew that the most important thing I could do would be to sit on my little meditation cushion and get quiet. I remembered the power that one man in Texas had and how it influenced me, and others in the group, and the effect that his inner peaceful attunement had on seemingly all of us. I realized that morning of 9/11 that my most important job on any day would be to get peaceful within: that my moments in meditation could be a real contribution not only to my own peacefulness but also to others on the planet.

That morning I felt a zeal to start a campaign of peace. What could a multitude of people accomplish by rising each day, getting quiet, and tuning in to their version of the "I am" presence?

* * *

The flip side is also true. Negative emotional contagion can operate like secondhand smoke. Someone who is emitting anger or holding a strongly negative charge influences those around him or her. You know this to be true because you've experienced it.

We are able to read some of what others are feeling and thinking, yet we may not recognize the secondhand effect of our own emotions on others. When we don't manage our stress response well, not only does our own health and wellbeing take a hit, but also we may leave others or our company/endeavors without leadership if a health crisis ensues. Negative emotional contagion occurs. We rob ourselves and others around us of the opportunity to harvest enjoyable work relationships and the fruits of ease, health, harmony, joy, vitality, and productivity.

* * *

Consider

- Who in your environment do you subject to stress when your own stress meter has been stuck in the on position for too long?

- What challenges would it create for your company, family, community, or coworkers if you had serious health issues, like a debilitating stroke or heart attack?
- How do you know when you're close to burnout?
- What are your telltale symptoms of unrelieved stress? Do you have mood changes, or do you distance yourself from others?
- Under what circumstances do you find almost everyone irritating? (This can be a signal of burnout.)

Setting limits on work and prioritizing self-care can be easier after an attention-getting health crisis. But why wait?

* * *

Reflecting on the questions above could lead you to a decision to overcome patterns of self-neglect, which, in turn, will prevent stress-related health consequences.

Summary of Chapter 4
We inhabit a fantastically designed, well-coordinated body-mind, capable of getting us out of acute danger. Our modern dangers are often complicated and chronic, seemingly never ending and often without easy or feasible solutions. Evaluating the contrast in our lives is important (such as whether we have enough pleasurable energy output with enough balancing rest/renewal and relaxation). Using energy fully (energy output) and then getting enough relaxation and rest yield healthy contrast that may prevent a prolonged stress response, burnout or depression.

STRESS AND WELLBEING: MANAGING STRESS DOES MATTER!

Next Steps - Putting it all together
So how do we cope? How can we preserve our health and prevent the ravages of a stress response stuck at "on"? Whether at work or at home, the peace-at-work process described in Chapter 2 reminds us that often we benefit from:

- Taking a pause to interrupt our automatic emotions and thoughts
- Noticing
- Using a skill to relax, shift or accept

Chapter 3 includes ten skills that may be useful to experiment with:

(1) Minibreaks: short breaks that can include inhaling to a count of four, holding for two, three, or four counts and exhaling for eight counts. You can also be belly breathing or repeating an uplifting phrase while breathing. Often done in the midst of life and work.

(2) EBT check-in tool: checking in on ourselves, like a good friend would, by taking a few intentional breaths, noticing the body, and making a few stretches or shifts to bring the body into balance, kindly observing thoughts/feelings without judgment. Can also include checking your brain state and accepting your state.

(3) Acceptance via "it's like this": a mindfulness tool that works by breathing, coming to the present moment awareness and then accepting what is as it is; accepting that, at this moment at least, "it's like

this." A seemingly simple practice that embodies all seven qualities of mindfulness.

(4) Yogic breathing: a deeper three-part breath that can be done while active or relaxing. During the three-part breath, the belly fills with air, then the midchest and upper chest. To exhale, empty the air from upper chest, middle chest, and, finally, the belly. Rapid abdominal breathing can clear emotions; it requires a little privacy and time to learn this skill.

(5) Fifty-breaths walk: this mind-body skill involves counting each breath as you walk outside. Aim to count fifty breaths as you walk outside and focus on the breathing and counting.

(6) Shifting perspectives: perception is often automatic for us and limits our choices. Playing with other ways to look at a current challenge can be done with the perspectives tool. It allows us to step outside the box of our own perceptions long enough to look at other alternatives. Use one or two of your own perspectives on the challenge then add another three to four that are possible or whimsical. Explore how you'd feel looking at the challenge in each perspective. See if it changes your response or offers any new options.

(7) Loving-kindness meditation: a series of five statements of positive intent that are first offered (or said) for oneself and then can be said for someone you love/care about, and possibly for a neutral or a difficult person.

(8) Prayer: spiritual dialogue that may take many forms.
(9) Claiming space and victorous stance: yoga-type physical movements that can shift personal or group energy beneficially. Pairing the breath with the movements is ideal.
(10) Meditation: listening within—can be done with a secular or spiritual focus. Often involves selecting a focus, such as the breath or a particular word, and then returning the mind to that breath or word when the mind wanders.

These 10 simple skills enhance the rest/renewal aspect of our nervous system (also called the parasympathetic system). The regular practice of mind-body skills has been shown to mitigate the chronic stress reaction and contribute to greater vitality, productivity, and wellbeing. Taking pauses to practice also increases the likelihood that we'll be present to notice and savor life's joyful moments.

Please pick one of the skills or practice challenges in the next chapter in order to integrate theory into practice.

V

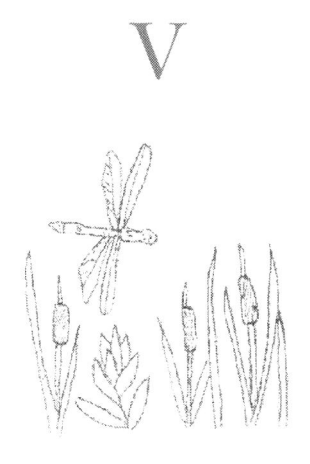

PRACTICE CHALLENGES

Reading about skills without practicing them is like visually admiring a bicycle without getting on it to experience the freedom and pleasure of movement. This section gives you four practice challenges. A practice challenge gives you the opportunity to try out (or practice) some of the skills in this book. You may elect to take all four or only one or two. If you're not sure, start with Practice Challenge 1.

Practice Challenge 1. Pick One Skill to Practice
You will pick one of the skills to practice.

Step 1: Establish your vision of wellbeing. (Answer any three of the following.)
What would you love to have in your life in the next month? In three months?
What would allow you to feel at your best? How do you feel at your best?

What's in your vision of thriving and flourishing?
What would a thriving leader look/feel/be like?
What has to happen for this to become a reality?
If you could be the person you want to be, what would others notice?
How would you feel? What would you notice?

Step 2: What are the values that are important as you develop greater wellbeing and stress resilience? Pause to evaluate why this matters.

Possible examples of values or desired outcomes:

- Feeling "in integrity" more of the time; "walking your talk"
- Having more energy, with less energy lost in nonproductive internal dialogue
- Having kindness to self and others
- Practicing a pause more often before reacting
- Being mindful: enjoying feeling present with coworkers, friends, and family more and more
- Mastering stress resilience skills
- Being healthy: less reliance on stress eating or drinking, spending, or working to excess
- Self-care that is like preventive self-maintenance
- Living a longer life, in better physical health: lower blood pressure, lower heart rate, and less back pain
- Boosting capacity for peak performance

Step 3: Pick one self-care resilience or stress-reduction tool to help you reach the vision or values you identified in step 1 or 2.

PRACTICE CHALLENGES

- 1—Minibreak
- 2—EBT Check-Ins
- 3—It's Like This
- 4—Rapid Abdominal Breathing
- 5—Fifty-Breaths Walk
- 6—Out of the Box—Shifting Perspective
- 7—Loving-Kindness
- 8—Prayer
- 9—Claiming Space and Victorious Stance
- 10—Meditation
- Other _____
- Scream in the Freezer

Steps 4 and 5 utilize the stages of change theory. (You will find a more complete guide on stages of change in chapter 6.)

In step 4, identify your stage of change. Look to the right-hand column to see the likely next tasks for your stage of change in step 5.

Step 4: Pick your stage of change for the skill you chose in step 3. (See the left column.)

<u>Stages of change</u>
- Contemplation

- Preparation

<u>Possible next tasks</u>
Evaluate benefits/risks of making the desired change.
List the steps of preparation
Ask yourself these preparation questions:
- Am I prepared to commit to this?

- Action
  - What hurdles need to be anticipated?
  - Time issues? Substitutions?
  - Have I really committed to this?

  You're beginning.
  You're doing it! Continue Serving as your own supporter. Outside support may also be useful.

- Recycling or relapse

  Recognizing a slipup.
  Review the importance of the change. What benefit was I getting when things were working?
  What important value(s) was I honoring before the slipup? With the slipup?
  Am I ready to be in the preparation stage again?

- Maintenance and evaluation

  Checking in with the behavior. How am I doing with this behavior? Has it become automatic? Do I need to tend to or modify it to ensure continued success?

Step 5. Gives you the practical translation of what to do for your current stage.

Step 6: Pick a small step to accomplish, setting it as a SMART goal, one that is Small, Measurable, Achievable, Realistic, and Timed or Target dated. Ask yourself how you will know when you achieve it. Test yourself to see if it's realistic and feasible.

Here's an example of this process:
Step 1. Vision: feeling vibrant and having plenty of energy
Step 2. Value of integrity, preventive self-care
Step 3. Skill: fifty-breaths walk
Step 4. Stage of change: contemplation or preparation
Step 5. Need to clarify benefits and do some planning for how to accomplish them
Step 6. SMART goal step: list two benefits that would come from accomplishing one fifty-breaths walk in the next week

My Six Steps
(1) Vision: _____.

(2) Values or desired outcomes:_____.

(3) The skill I want to practice is_____.

(4) My stage of change on this is_____.

(5) What I need to do for my stage of change is_____.

(6) My small step or SMART goal is _____.

Remember to celebrate success each time.

Know that you can repeat this practice challenge using another of the skills in the book.

Practice Challenge 2. What Do I Want? What Is Important to Me?
Sometimes we really need something that takes our breath away to be a large enough goal or challenge. What would your big-enough challenge be?

As an example, my stress-resilience wellness aim is to get through the most difficult part of the work year in the fall without weight gain. To accomplish this, I need something big and specific enough to be a worthy challenge. I decided that my big-enough challenge is to get some movement every day at work or at home (twenty-minute walk at least five days/week) and increase the frequency of bodywork (massage or reflexology weekly) during this eight- to ten-week period. I like rewards (don't we all?), so in setting up this challenge, I give myself the reward of some fresh flowers for my desk at the beginning of each week after I've met the challenge.

Practice Challenge 3. Partnering with Yourself to Become Your Own Health Coach
Pick a skill from the book you want to focus on, such as having a longer fuse at work or at home or taking a fifty-breaths walk to stay more alert and in better shape at work.

Self-Coaching: Taking Action Form

(1) Write your focus/personal aim.
(2) What are the benefits? Write one on each of the outer lines.

(3) What strategies could help you with your aim? Write these down, even if they seem silly, playful, or unreasonable!
(4) Write in some of your strengths or past experiences that will help you.
(5) What will you need to reach your aim?
(6) What are the barriers or roadblocks? These are the things that you'll need to reckon with before it's possible to move forward.
(7) Do you need support outside of yourself? Support might come from a person, from a part of yourself, or even from a group or professional. What would this support be?

Take a moment to appreciate that you've set up a great foundation by doing these seven steps! Where will you go from here? If you were going to take a tiny step, what would it be? Is there a way to pair that small step with something else you'd be doing anyway? See the blank form below and in the appendix.

Self-Coaching: Live, Love, Lead
This form is used for some do-it-yourself personal coaching

1. Focus/personal aim
_____

2. Benefits	3. Strategies	4. Strengths
_____	_____	_____
_____	_____	_____
_____	_____	_____
_____	_____	_____

5. What's needed?   6. Barriers/hurdles?

_____   _____

_____   _____

_____   _____

_____   _____

7. What support will I need (from myself, others)?

_____

_____

Practice Challenge 4. Monitoring and Evaluating Your Progress

Having an accountability buddy helps with success. Pen-and-paper tracking or using an app or calendar also serves as a success booster.

Is there a way to track my small steps that feels beneficial?
How will I measure success?
Do I need support? (Hint: Most all of us do.)

Personal Story

I enjoy life more when I've had time to be creative, when I've have had at least two trips to the gym each week, and when I meditate in the morning. Since gym visits and meditation are practices that have mostly become habits, my focus now is building the practice of having writing appointments that I keep each week and month. I treasure time for journaling, creative writing, and editing/completing writing projects. So in addition to documenting the times I plan to do creative writing or editing on my calendar, I'm following up to track the writing time I actually accomplish via a chart on my laptop computer. It allows me to track my progress from almost anywhere.

VI

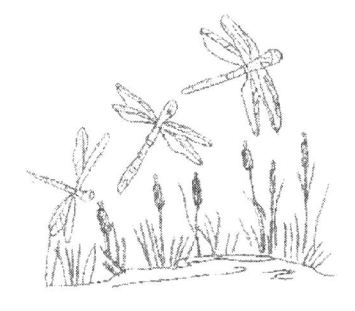

SWERVING TOWARD HEALTH: HOW CHANGE HAPPENS

In this chapter, we'll explore your readiness to use the skills in this book. If you've tried one or two of the skills already, or taken some of the practice challenges, you may be wondering, "How can I convert this new skill into something that is part of my permanent stress-management tool kit?" This little mini assessment can serve as an inventory of where you are now in relation to where you'd like to be.

The part of this chapter titled "The Process of Change" gives you a look at some of the masters of change and successful approaches to making change. If the only reason you picked up this book is to learn some new stress-management skills, but you are already good at incorporating new behaviors (or extinguishing things you're ready to let go), you may want to skip over this chapter. However, if you want to convert the one-time trial of a new skill into a useful habit, this chapter may be useful.

Wouldn't it be great to have fewer stressful moments and more wellbeing? Even with a robust longing and vision for wellbeing, it's still difficult to actualize your vision. Making a plan, setting small goals, and changing behavior is often required, and usually change isn't easy. When you've made a change that was helpful and durable, how did it happen? What do you know about yourself and how you best add or delete a behavior?

Current Assessment: Stress and Building Stress Resilience
Note: If you completed the short earlier version of this checklist, you may want to take it again here to see whether things have changed. (There is no right answer. Being human, we may hold several competing views at the same time. You can pick more than one.)

- I don't consciously think I'm stressed but often have physical symptoms that are typically associated with stress (such as a tense neck or cold hands).
- It's hard to make changes or even know where to begin.
- I'm too busy to consider stress and how I handle it.
- Even thinking about stress or the next steps for health is boring.
- I attend workshops but have a hard time putting anything into practice.
- I've never thought much about the effects of stress on my health/well-being.

- I've been helping myself by getting better sleep, eating well, exercising, or _____.
- With every little healthy choice I make, it gets easier.
- I'm eager to begin practicing these skills, or I have already begun to _____.
- I'm thinking about _____.
- I feel proud that I've started _____ again.
- I feel proud that I've tried out this new skill: _____.
- It shouldn't be so difficult to just do it, and yet I'm not doing it. Though I know I will in the future, right now I'm under stress, and it's not the right time for change.
- I experimented with practice challenge number _____.
- I know how to meditate, and I enjoy yoga when I get there. I now recognize that there is a cost to me when I don't prioritize these types of self-care activities.
- I manage stress much better than in the past.
- I know my setups and triggers for stress.

What do you notice about things you checked?
Have you already taken some ownership of your own health and in building your stress-resilience tool kit?
When you've made a change in the past, who or what helped you make the change?
What experiments or prior life experience prepared you to quit a habit or make a change?

Perhaps you have had difficulty making the changes you wanted to make. Sometimes appreciating all that's led to the present is part of the celebration and the preparation for taking the next step.

Personal Story

I had very high fitness standards for myself in my twenties. I remember going to the YES! health center in Washington, DC, where a wellness-oriented physician advised me that my expectations about fitness and self-care weren't reasonable. In my mind, running, yoga, and other pursuits needed to happen very regularly for me to feel halfway good about myself. My level of fitness was a marker for me for looking good enough, being attractive, and fitting in with the people and groups I wanted to belong to. I was letting a desire for a specific level of fitness and body shape dominate my life and undermine my self-worth in an unhealthy way.

In my thirties and forties, I continued to be fitness aware, but I grew to treasure peace of mind, self-worth, joy, and a deeper connection with the Divine even more than meeting my size or fitness quotient. I realized I could have these inner feel-good experiences without being perfect in my fitness regimen. So the gifts of my early life and drive for fitness and beauty weren't lost or unfounded; they were part of the journey of finding deeper joy. The change I started with pointed the way to a truer need with even more benefit. Along the way, it was no longer useful to have my self-love or self-worth be contingent upon meeting external goals.

Today I am still learning how to set reasonable expectations about the process of behavioral change, both for myself and with others. Recently I've enjoyed playing with the idea that I can expect or plan for an ideal day, and yet I live in real days, and planning for my real life and real days may be saner. I am learning to practice kindness, even as I also make progress toward my aims and goals.

I appreciate that wherever I am in the process of change, it counts. Today I do not terrorize myself with guilt and thinking I'm "not enough." Today, I usually have mercy on myself as I also keep an eye on my healthful aims. While I set goals, I'm also patient with the time frame for realizing goals.

Let's explore where you are now and where you'd like to be.

What is known about how people make change happen? What is the best way to move from one's present to realizing more health, vitality, and productivity?

The Process of Change
The people mentioned in this section are some of the pioneers in the field of health-behavior change. One of the contributions from Dr. Travis that I appreciate is his visual model, the Illness-Wellness Continuum. He also names the steps toward optimal wellness. Since these steps mirror my experience, I value his map of how change can occur. The

Illness-Wellness Continuum gives me a road map for wellbeing and a way to assess where I am, and it directs where I could go.

John W. Travis, MD, **MPH,** coauthored the *Wellness Workbook.* He is one of the fathers of the wellness movement in the United States. He depicts health and wellbeing on a continuum from illness to optimal wellness. Traditional health care (the treatment paradigm) moves us from illness to a neutral point we call "health," but it doesn't address optimum wellbeing. The process of moving toward wellness often includes:

- Awareness. Examples include taking inventory of the area(s) of your health you want to change.
- Education. Learning steps include experimenting with new skills or seeking out knowledge before implementing a change.
- Growth and change. Choosing small changes leads to long-term wellbeing. Take tiny steps, gain confidence, and choose another step to build success.

Wellness is a process—never a static state.

This model shows the relationship of the wellness and treatment paradigms. Moving from the center to the left shows a progressively worsening state of health. Moving to the right of center indicates increasing levels of health and wellbeing.

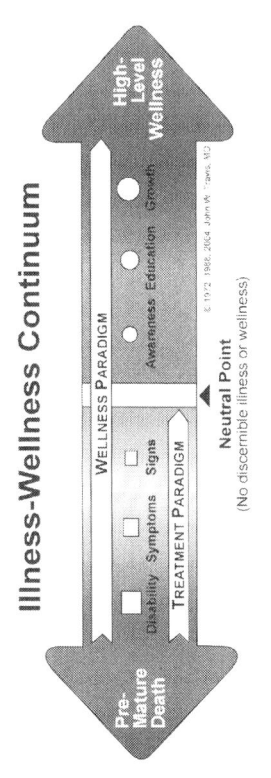

Figure 6.1. Illness-Wellness Continuum by John W. Travis, MD.

If you've ever taken a health risk assessment (HRA) or offered an HRA to your employees, you will recognize that it generally measures only the left hand side of the diagram, that is, treatment-model factors of health or illness. The beauty of this model is that it includes a focus on optimum health, or high-level wellness. John W. Travis, *Wellness Workbook*. Celestial Arts, 2004.

Keep in mind that symptoms are the things you see that the doctor doesn't yet: more frequent headaches, body aches or backaches, more frequent urination after eating sweets, etc.

Signs are things the doctor sees and can measure, such as elevated blood pressure or higher-than-normal glucose. Often symptoms show up long before the signs of disease. If we take action to address the signs or symptoms, we can reverse the trend toward illness or disease and move in the direction of optimum health. No matter where a person is on the Illness-Wellness Continuum, it's never too late to move toward optimum wellness! One of the messages for me in these models and in Dr. Travis's work is it's never too late to change and move toward greater well-being, but also that small steps in awareness can lead the way to substantial beneficial change.

The Wellness Inventory Program, an extension of the work of Dr. Travis, is an online self-assessment of wellness that includes an extensive set of tools for making improvements that you discover you'd like to implement. The inventory/self-assessment and options for enhancing wellness are available at http://www.wellpeople.com or through the Hygeia Center for Wellbeing website http://www.hygeiacenter.com.

* * *

I also value the transtheoretical model, or stages of change theory, of James Prochaska, PhD, and Carlo DiClemente, PhD. They have named the steps that most of us progress through as we move from thinking about something to doing it. What I value most about their work is, first, they provide a map of change that seems reasonable, in my experience, and, second, there is an innate trust that even when we feel stuck, we're always somewhere in the process of change. They note the importance of preparation as a stage of change that is necessary for success. Since I skip this stage at times and then wonder why I don't succeed, I think there is still a lot for me to learn here.

Prochaska and DiClemente developed the stages of change theory for health care settings. They identified six change stages. To better understand their model, I suggest you pick one of the following examples of something you would like to or have changed as you read about these six stages of change.

I'd like to…(pick one):

- ✓ eat leafy greens like spinach or kale three times a week
- ✓ eat two fruits and three vegetables most days
- ✓ get fifteen more minutes or more of exercise most days
- ✓ stop smoking
- ✓ start getting up every hour to interrupt sedentary time
- ✓ get seven to eight hours of sleep most nights
- ✓ floss daily
- ✓ limit screen time after 10:00 p.m. or an hour before bedtime
- ✓ clear my desk or workplace for fifteen minutes before I leave work
- ✓ offer one positive comment to a coworker or family member daily
- ✓ spend five minutes planning for the next day before leaving work

- ✓ take a minibreak twice a day
- ✓ take a fifty-breaths walk twice a week

Got one? Keep this item in mind as we look at the stages we go through in making change:

- Precontemplation—I don't care, am not interested, don't want to consider. I dismiss or discount this possibility, and am really not interested now.
- Contemplation—I am noticing what others are doing. I am not too interested, but am aware of the value of the behavior. I'm drawn to my usual pattern.
- Preparation—I have decided it would be useful to make the change. I don't yet have the skills or knowledge needed to change to the new behavior. I may need support. I may need knowledge or to develop some new skill. I can prepare for change. At this stage it's helpful to identify and take ultrasmall steps to progress to the next stage successfully.
- Action—I have begun to take steps of preparation and to practice the activity. I feel the success of small accomplishments and I am in the change zone some of the time.
- Maintenance and evaluation—I do this now, and it's not a struggle. I am tending to the new behavior. I notice when I get off track, and I get back to what matters. Changes are more automatic; it takes less effort to maintain the change than it did before.
- Recycling or relapse—I've had a slipup or a period of recycling back into earlier behaviors. I return to the desired behavior when I'm ready. (In this stage,

> a person may return to one of the earlier stages of change—contemplation, preparation, or action—when he or she refocuses after the lapse.)

Now recall the item of change you selected and place yourself in one of the stages of change. Which stage of change are you in?

There is an inherent kindness in the work of Prochaska and DiClemente. Recognizing the stage we are in helps stop the inner finger wagging. We can give the harsh inner critic or inner gremlin voices a miss. We can skip past the inner critic that often zaps our energy. In this view, excuses are actually informative; they are an indication that we're still in a contemplation or preparation stage—not yet ready to make a change. For some internal or external reason, we may need to explore the belief that is in the way, set up a substitute substance or activity, make a plan, or explore our ambivalence about the change. Taking the time to celebrate any step we do make is recommended!

In the stages of change theory, it's recognized that we can let go of the tyranny that suggests the action step is the only step that counts. There is no blame, shame, or moral judgment regarding the stage of change we're in. The stages of change theory really does allow us to breathe in our own air more fully. There are simply steps to take that fit with where we are. Research shows that making a change is actually much more feasible and successful under these circumstances.

I've accompanied clients as a health-change facilitator for more than thirty years. Even though I've had lots of exposure to the stages of change theory, I am still learning how it can be helpful in supporting changes in behavior—mine and others'.

For example, there are a couple of watch points:

(1) Commitment is an important step before starting to change. If my commitment is not yet solid (if I'm still hesitant or feeling in conflict about some change or health strategy I'm considering), it is best to pause and explore the ambivalence about making a change, rather than to attempt or start taking action. People who are in the late-contemplation stage—aware of the benefits but not really committed—often relapse if they don't commit first and support that commitment with adequate preparation.

(2) The preparation stage is the most easily skipped over, since many of us are primed to get results by taking action quickly. Yet this preparatory stage predicts long-term success. It is important to take time and consider the preparation needed. Preparation and planning for issues such as time, costs, barriers, substitutes, strategies, and necessary support are best anticipated before proceeding. More often than not, the people who skip over the preparation and planning stage will find themselves in the relapse or recycling stage. There is nothing wrong with relapse or recycling; however, repeated visits to this stage can bring a feeling of going in circles and delay getting to goal.

* * *

SWERVING TOWARD HEALTH: HOW CHANGE HAPPENS

What I love about the stages of change theory is the encouragement to take it one stage at a time. There is no need to jump from the first idea (contemplation) to completion (action or evaluation). We can give ourselves the benefit of starting when we're ready. We can support our own success by listing and experimenting with preparation steps. We can trust that if we're feeling resistance to change, there are good reasons that we need to uncover. This framework invites us to trust ourselves and take the time to move some of the barriers out of the way before stepping into the action stage.

Which stage of change is he in? How about the action stage?

In order to arrive successfully, he contemplated (thought about it) and planned (took small preparatory steps) to ultimately succeed in arriving safely on the roof.

As an example, do you remember when you learned that eating lots of vegetables would be best for health? Where are you now on that issue? Even though you may not get the recommended two to three cups per day, eating more vegetables is on your radar. Did you move, little by little, even over the course of years, to the place where you seldom have a day without vegetables? Using this or a similar example, you can see and measure your progress through the stages of change.

* * *

I have less direct experience with the work of Dr. Bandura; however, I've observed some of the things he references in his theories, such as that the company we keep in life has a big role to play in whether or not we're able to complete things we start, and make the changes we wish to make.

Albert Bandura, PhD, professor emeritus in psychology at Stanford, developed social learning theory. In this framework, successful changes are more likely to occur in a social network or in relationships with others. We are social mammals and are imitative by nature. We are more likely to do what we see others doing.

In addition to his work on the powerful influence of imitation, Bandura's research highlights self-efficacy: the idea that the more confident we are in our abilities, the more likely we are to be successful. This concept of self-efficacy ties in beautifully with the work of B. J. Fogg, another Stanford professor on behavioral change. According to Fogg, if we tackle small-enough steps, we're more likely to experience the "I can do this" sense of self-efficacy. Each small step we accomplish can be the preparation or trigger for the next small step. Each small step moves us toward a personal longer-term goal.

* * *

I was introduced to B. J. Fogg in August 2013 at a conference in Philadelphia. Any guy who would model his theory by doing push-ups on stage in front of thousands deserves to be included here. His research is on the cutting edge of how effective change happens. The lesson for me in his work is that when I set a very small goal that I can achieve (like doing 1 EBT check-in per day), it's likely I'll also move along and accomplish the bigger goal of, say, accomplishing five daily EBT check-ins and boosting stress resilience.

B. J. Fogg is the director of the Persuasive Tech Lab at Stanford University. His research identified that people build success when they take a tiny step within their ability—a small step that does not require a high level of motivation. Although having a trigger to start the action is important, one step, when successfully completed, becomes the trigger for the next small step. (Another way of describing a trigger is as an initiating event.)

* * *

Accountability also helps with successful behavioral change. Integrative health coaching is a process of empowering people in making meaningful changes in their wellbeing. The designed alliance between individuals (coach and client) creates a remarkably effective container for growth and change. Integrative health coaching is built on the idea that people have innate wisdom, strength, and creativity, and, when their own assets are skillfully recruited, these things will guide them toward health more effectively than external or expert advice. Health coaches act as part of the health care team to aid clients in clarifying their own vision of health and in providing accountability. Health coaches act as a guide through the process of change.

One of the things I love about the health-coaching process is that it's a skillful method for overcoming both the external barriers to change we're aware of (time/ability/physical constraints) as well as the internal barriers we often ignore of thought, belief, and attitude. Having coaching support can make accomplishing your goals much more fun, as well as more likely. Duke-certified integrative health coaches, Wellcoach-trained coaches, and coaches trained to deliver the Wellness Inventory all can be recommended.

Have Mercy

For those who strive, sometimes good isn't enough. It is important to recognize the suffering that striving can create. Even worthy goals can set us up for striving and self-judging. Unless we stay in a curious and trusting place, even positive ambitions for self-care can turn cloudy with judging and measuring.

Stephen Levine is a remarkable teacher of mindfulness. His influence helped me to open myself to grace and some letting go of inner harshness.

> Have mercy! Have mercy on you.
>
> (Stephen Levine, Omega Institute Workshop)

Know that you're on the path, and even being present with awareness and mercy is a huge step in self-transformation. We can be so hard on ourselves in this culture. Please allow the shoulds and musts to be like birds. Keep walking toward peace and a release from stressful reactions. Let the birds fly by.

APPENDIX

Forms:
1. Perspectives Form

Name the issue

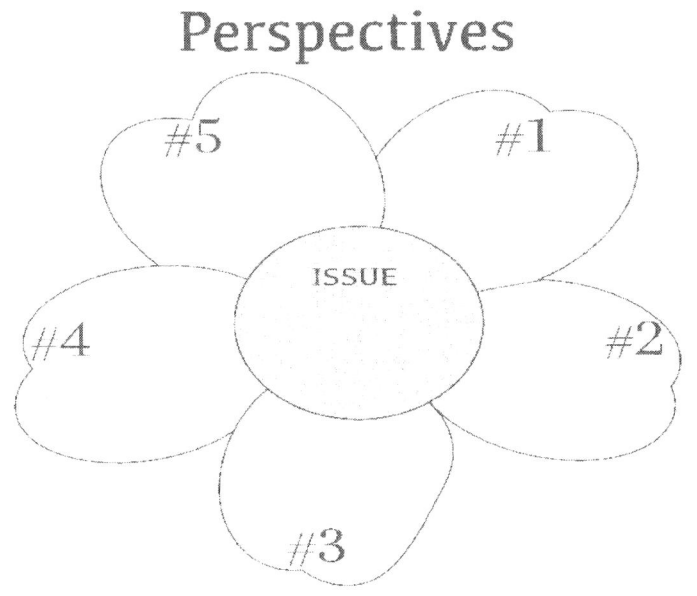

Perspectives

1–5 Possible perspectives or vantage points for dealing with the issue

Explore each possible perspective via the questions

Questions to ask of/in each perspective
If this perspective had a color, what would the color be?
How do I feel in this perspective?
What would be possible in this perspective?
Do I want to move toward or away from this?

2. Self-Coaching: Live, Love, Lead
This form is used for some do-it-yourself personal coaching

1. Focus/personal aim
_____

2. Benefits	3. Strategies	4. Strengths
_____	_____	_____
_____	_____	_____
_____	_____	_____

5. What's needed?   6. Barriers/hurdles?

7. What support will I need (from myself, others)?
_____
_____

ENDNOTES AND RESOURCES

Chapter 3. Ten Simple Skills

Skill 2. The EBT Check-In Tool
For a quick introduction to EBT, I recommend you go to www.ebtgroups.com or read the book *Wired for Joy*, by Laurel Mellin.

A good starting place is to enroll in an EBT Basics *Wired for Joy* course. The EBT Basics or EBT Connect training starts the process of rewiring the brain's emotional set point by giving participants an introduction to the tools that correspond to the five brain states. Training includes learning how to do an EBT cycle; this is the power tool of the method.

> Most of us have a brain with some stuck-in-stress circuits. There are times when our response is disproportionate to the actual event or experience. To revamp these circuits, longer-term practice of EBT is beneficial. After the initial eight-week course, additional EBT workbooks and courses can help individuals to rewire toward more beneficial patterns. You may find survival circuits as you practice these skills. The tools to identify, negate, and transform these survival circuits into something vastly more beneficial are also included in the intermediate or advanced EBT training. Mobile apps and other means of support are available to facilitate EBT check-ins and boost the effective use of the tools for stress resilience.

Skill 3. Acceptance: "It's Like This"
Dr. Jeffrey and Mary Brantley's comprehensive guide on mindfulness can be found on their CD, available through Duke Integrative Medicine, and their mindfulness-based stress reduction (MBSR) programs at dukeintegrativemedicine.org or by calling 1-866-313-0959. Ask for the Duke Integrative Medicine MBSR CD series.

Skill 4. Yogic Breathing Practices
If you would like supervision and support learning the breathing practices in chapter 3, please seek out an integral yoga instructor. Other hatha yoga instructors may also be able to guide your practice.

For a list of certified integral yoga instructors, go to http://iyta.org/teachers-directory.

Skill 6. Out of the Box—Shifting Perspective
Just a few minutes with *Peace is Every Step*, by Thich Nhat Hanh, over a lunch or break can effect a change in perspective.

See the blank form and the example of perspectives work in the appendix.

Skill 7. Loving-Kindness, Peace, and Harmony
For further reading:

Sharon Salzburg. *Lovingkindness: The Revolutionary Art of Happiness*. Shambhala Classics, 2002.

Sharon Salzburg. *Real Happiness at Work*. Workman Publishing Company Inc., 2013.

Skill 8. Prayer
A Course in Miracles, Workbook for Students. Foundation for Inner Peace, 1976.

Barbara Fredrickson. *Positivity.* Random House, 2009. Visit www.positivityratio.com/single.php to assess your positivity ratio. Recognize that your positivity score will change from day to day since emotions are fluid.

Brother Lawrence. *The Practice of the Presence of God*, various editions.

Daily Word, a Unity School of Christianity publication: visit www.dailyword.com or call 800-669-0282.

The Unity School of Christianity in Missouri offers a 24/7 prayer line. You can call Silent Unity at 1-800-669-2000 or visit www.silentunity.org. All prayer requests are treated with reverence and confidentiality. Prayers continue on the issue you request for thirty days.

Skill 9. Claiming Space and Victorious Stance
Swami Shivapremananda. *Yoga for Stress Relief.* New York: Random House, 1997.

Skill 10. Meditation
Ananda Sangha Worldwide: www.ananda.org; (530) 478-7560.

Jon Kabat-Zinn. *Full Catastrophe Living: Using the Wisdom of Your Body and Mind to Face Stress, Pain, and Illness.* Random House, 2013. Outlines a twelve-week program aimed at reducing the effects of stress. Books and audio recordings by Jon Kabat-Zinn are excellent ways to gain an introduction to mindfulness meditation. Dr. Kabat-Zinn did the research that led to the development of mindfulness-based stress-reduction programs.

Mindfulness-based stress-reduction programs (MBSR) are offered now in many medical-center settings nationally.

Mindfulness-based stress-reduction program CDs (Duke Integrative Medicine, with Dr. Jeffrey and Mary Brantley) are available at dukeintegrativemedicine.org or by calling 1-866-313-0959.

Self-Realization Fellowship: www.yogananda-SRF.org; (323) 225-2471. SRF offers a complete course of meditation instruction and guidance for healthful living via the lessons by Paramahansa Yogananda.

Yoga nidra meditation, Hygeia Center for Wellbeing: http://www.hygeiacenter.com/Services/QuietingtheMind.aspx

Chapter 6. Swerving Toward Health: How Change Happens
For more information about B. J. Fogg and related research, see behaviorgrid.org or behaviorwizard.org.

Stephen Levine, workshop leader at Omega Institute in 1987. Author of *A Gradual Awakening*. Anchor, 1989, and *Who Dies?* Gill & MacMillan, 2000.

REFERENCES

Chapter 3

T. L. Jacobs, E. S. Epel, and J. Lin. "Intensive Meditation Training, Immune Cell Telomerase Activity, and Psychological Mediators." *Psychoneuroendocrinology*, 2011. 36 (5): 664–81.

S. Satchidananda. *The Yoga Sutras of Patanjali*. Virginia: Integral Yoga Publications, 1978, 2011. p. 19–20.

Chapter 4

James W. Kalat. *Biological Psychology*, 9th edition. Thomson Wadsworth, 2007. p. 575.

V. S. Ramachandran. *The Telltale Brain: A Neuroscientist's Quest for What Makes Us Human*. New York: W. W. Norton & Company, 2011. p. xv.

ABOUT THE AUTHOR

Cynthia L. Moore MS, RDN, CDE, FAND works at the University of Virginia Nutrition Counseling Center and Integrative Medicine clinic, in addition to the Hygeia Center. Her past work has included many areas of preventive medicine, research and nutrition, education, and therapy, in settings including teaching hospitals, colleges, medical schools, resorts/spas, and a preventive diagnostic clinic. She holds degrees in nutrition and has worked as a registered dietitian/nutritionist and certified diabetes educator, faculty instructor, integrative health coach, leader, and speaker. In addition to her ongoing work as a manager, nutritionist, and provider of emotional brain training, she continues to develop programs and workshops on well-being, yoga, and stress management. She is the catalyst and founding director of The Hygeia Project and the Hygeia Center for Wellbeing.

The Hygeia Project offers experiential education in integrative health and self-care. Hygeia was the Greek goddess of mental and physical health and the daughter of Asclepius, the Greek father of medicine. The Hygeia domain in the ancient healing temples of Asclepius was health and the prevention of illness through diet, pure water, sleep, dreaming, and exercise. In modern times, self-care practices are in the Hygeia domain (including adequate rest, nourishment, movement, and satisfying work-life balance).

The Hygeia Center for Wellbeing is in development as an online resource for building personal self-health-care skills, including stress resilience, nutrition studio, and skills to quiet the mind. The Hygeia Center will offer self-care learning opportunities, links to integrative health coaching, and health self-assessments, including the multidimensional online Wellness Inventory. See www.hygeiacenter.com for audio and other links to some of the skills in *Live, Love, Lead*.

The Margery & Robin Williams Fund is the charitable arm of the Hygeia Project and makes the Hygeia Center offerings more widely available to those who live with mental-health concerns.

Made in the USA
Middletown, DE
03 June 2017